FORCE MAJEURE

FORCE MAJEURE

A futurist's guide to boldly thriving on your terms in the future of work

Dr. Terri Horton MBA, MA, SHRM-CP, PHR, SWP
Workforce Futurist

Force Majeure

Publisher:
Dr. Terri Horton

Publishing consultant:
Professional Woman Publishing, LLC
www.pwnbooks.com

ISBN: 978-0-578-24971-1

This book is dedicated to those who fearlessly run towards the future and have the courage to boldly design it on their own terms.

CONTENTS

Acknowledgements ix

Introduction xi

1 Force Majeure **1**
The Unfolding of the Future of Work Will Be a Force Majeure for Most

2 The Covid-Altered Future Of Work **17**
The Path Forward 2020–2030

3 Be Emotionally Intelligent And Resilient **23**
The Post-Covid-19 Power Currencies

4 Be Hyper-Relevant **41**
Think, Act, Perform Like a Futurist and Collect Your Receipts

5 Be Audaciously Bold **63**
Unapologetically Pursue New and Reimagined Possibilities

6 Thrive On Your Terms **79**
Thriving on Your Terms Is Your Power and Your Future

7 Your Thrive Plan **97**
No Force Majeure Clause in the Future of Work – Live Your Plan

Notes 103

About The Author 113

ACKNOWLEDGEMENTS

I would like to thank my family, friends and colleagues who supported me through this project and who believed in the power of my story, the value of my insights, and my ability to positively impact the lives of others.

force ma·jeure

an unexpected, uncontrollable, and disruptive event

"For most workers today, the unfolding of the future of work, particularly, between 2021-2030 will be a series of disruptive, unanticipated, and uncontrollable events. It will be their force majeure."

—Dr. Terri Horton—

INTRODUCTION

I remember the first time I read a contractual force majeure clause. It was on the contract I received for my first large-five-figure consulting client. Simply put, the clause excused both parties from liability in the event of a disruptive, unforeseen, or unavoidable circumstance or occurrence. It was the largest contract I had received to date, and I definitely did not want anything to trigger the clause and prevent me from delivering for the client and collecting my fee. No earthquakes, no acts of civil or military authority, let alone an act of God or anything else that I could not imagine at the time. You get the picture.

Let me set the stage for you as I continue. You see, I am a workforce futurist, and my expertise sits at the intersection of the future of work, artificial intelligence, and the impact on organizations and people. This intersection of the future of work and artificial intelligence by nature are disruptive and unavoidable. So, as I signed the contract, I reflected on the irony of the clause in the context of my work as a futurist responsible for providing clients with foresight and strategies to navigate disruption, the unforeseen and to thrive in the future of work. I realized then that the unfolding of the future of work in and of itself could trigger a force majeure for many. It had the potential to abruptly and radically change or even potentially cancel what we view as conventional social and employment contracts and even safety nets relied on for decades. It could trigger abrupt shifts in organizational structures, business and people strategy, careers, how we live, and how we define both success and thriving.

Let me amplify this a bit for you and provide more threading and texture around impact. Examples of shifts in organizational structures that align with the demands of the future of work are the shifts from traditional hierarchies to collaborative networks and ecosystems anchored in digitalization, cloud-based infrastructure, and artificial intelligence. Examples of shifts in business strategy aligned with the demands of the future of work are the shifts to more agile, future-focused adaptive cultures that are human-centered, growth and customer focused, data-driven, and highly responsive to market, competitive, and customer shifts and demands. Examples of shifts in people strategy include:

- how talent is recruited, assessed, ranked, and acquired using artificial intelligence, neuroscience, natural language processing, biometric and psychometric analysis
- how jobs, work, tasks, and hybrid skill requirements are redesigned and augmented by artificial intelligence
- how employees are trained and developed using personalized adaptive learning platforms and predictive analytics
- how performance is tracked, and evaluated by AI productivity platforms that assess work quality, distractions, and time management
- how organizational design and mobility drive remote and hybrid work decisions
- how employee engagement is assessed to identify happiness, collaboration, inclusivity, and disengagement
- how worker experience is humanized

Future of work business and people strategies are grounded in enabling organizations and workers to thrive! Now do you understand how the future of work can be disruptive, unforeseen, and a force majeure that voids the ideas, and expectations that workers have of their employers, their jobs, and their careers for those who are not prepared? It is for this reason that I titled the book Force Majeure and use the term as a metaphor for a series of disruptive and triggering events in the unfolding of the future of work that may render void the metaphoric contract you believe you have with the future of work.

The COVID-19 pandemic proved to be a force majeure for nearly every aspect of our lives. It was disruptive, unforeseen and the consequences were vast. In some cases, unavoidable. It changed our consumer behavior, how we socialized, facilitated the explosive growth of e-commerce and the touchless economy, amplified inequalities in healthcare, raised awareness and elevated the national conversation on mental health and altered when, where, and how we worked. The COVID-19 pandemic was the force majeure of our lifetime and showed us how quickly and inhospitably a disruptive force can change everything. Therefore, as the COVID-altered future of work continues to reveal itself, we need a roadmap for navigating the new realities of business, work, and careers.

It doesn't matter if you are an executive, consultant, mid-career manager, budding supervisor, individual contributor, or recent college graduate. We all must come to terms with how we will approach the potential second force majeure of this decade. The second force majeure I am referring to, is the fundamental disruption of jobs and careers driven by AI and the impact of the COVID-19 pandemic on how we work. We must contemplate and understand how our industries, organizations, roles, and careers will be impacted by accelerated digital transformation and shifts in both business and people strategies. We must harness the resolve to lead, shift paradigms, work through volatility, uncertainty, complexity, ambiguity and somehow learn to continuously shift and pivot as we reskill, repurpose, and frequently reinvent our professional brands. All of this can be both challenging and unsettling. I know, because not only have I done it myself and trained and coached executives on the future of work before and during the pandemic, but I also spent years researching the impact of the future of work while completing my doctorate at the University of Southern California. My job is to help you move out of challenging and unsettling spaces and into spaces that empower you to move boldly ahead of the pace of transformation so that the rapid evolution of the future of work does not become your force majeure and you can thrive on your terms.

Research suggests that the COVID-19 pandemic accelerated the future of work by nearly a decade. Yes, a decade! The impact of social distancing and the subsequent labor market and economic fallout along with unprecedented civil unrest and political volatility triggered profound enterprise crisis management strategies to mitigate the devastating effects on business continuity, financials, brand strategy, equity, and sustainability. These strategies accelerated the implementation of AI systems and platforms, the redesign of organizational structures and business models, remote work, and leadership expectations at a pace that forced many to struggle just to keep up. Moving forward, thriving in the future of work on your terms requires that you rethink what it means to be resilient, relevant, and bold from a new perspective, with new strategies, an invigorated sense of urgency, and an unapologetic desire to design and define your success.

As the future of work continues to unfurl at an unmatched pace, it will be extraordinarily disruptive for organizations and workers who are not prepared. The impact will be unforeseen, unavoidable, and devastating for those who lack resilience, adaptability, relevancy, and a risk appetite for audacious boldness. It will be their force majeure. Conversely, those with actionable foresight and preparation can reimagine their future and adopt the right mindset and strategies that position them to think differently, and to leverage ingenuity to create new and innovative opportunities, over and over again, as they move boldly and thrive through 2030.

I wrote this book because wherever you are in your career, I want you to look the future of work squarely in the face and *own it on your terms* as we move through this decade. I will share my story, insights, provide you with specific strategies and actions for navigating the new next in the future of work. Don't let the future of work be your force majeure – Let's thrive on our terms together!

1
FORCE MAJEURE

The Unfolding of The Future of Work Will Be A Force Majeure for Most

"The 'roaring 2020s' have started with a force:
a pandemic that will propel us into the future
of work faster than expected."

—Forrester, 2020—

My Journey in Avoiding A Force Majeure

I have always been fascinated with trends, what's next, and the future ever since I can remember, so it's no wonder that I became a futurist in the second half of my career. I spent the first half of my career in the media industry. I held a variety of marketing and advertising management and executive positions across print, television, and online platforms with national and global media organizations. After 20 years in the industry and watching it contract under the weight of digitalization, I decided to pivot, reinvent, and launch my consulting practice to guide clients in developing strong sustainable brands.

Years later, during the Great Recession, as I watched multiple industries contract, the unemployment rate in the US soar, millions of workers become displaced, and the war for talent fiercely accelerate, I knew that the relationship between employers and workers would never be the same. So, I pivoted again to focus the business on employer branding, professional development, and executive coaching. This shift proved to be the catalyst for moving me into workforce futurism. My passion for staying ahead of the future and becoming an expert on the future of work enabled me to remain relentlessly focused on how organizations, work, learning, and people strategy would be reframed between 2020 and 2030. The same passion for staying ahead of the future and solidifying my expertise led me back to school to complete a doctorate at the University of Southern California, despite having two master's degrees and several industry credentials.

I strategically centered my research on the future of work, AI, skills, learning, and people strategy. As if that were not enough, since I did not have a traditional STEM background, am a woman of color, and had just turned 50 years old, I knew that my transition into workforce futurism might be challenged. So, to mitigate any potential challenges, I concurrently completed micro-credentials from the Massachusetts Institute of Technology in artificial intelligence business strategy and Cornell University in data analytics.

I'll admit it was a heavy lift. But I knew that by doing all of it, my background, experience, and credentials would clear the way for me to be glowingly positioned to thrive in what is now the future of work and lead others through the disruptive and exciting journey. What I want you to take-away from this chapter is that while uncertain, the future of work does not have to be a force majeure that disrupts and displaces you temporarily or permanently. You can and must shift, pivot, continuously learn, develop hybrid skills, and even reinvent if you plan to own this journey.

Think about this, within the first six months of 2020, we faced a global pandemic, social isolation, Great Depression-era unemployment, a social justice movement and political unrest all at once. All of these events profoundly affected and accelerated the unfolding of the future of work by nearly a decade. This acceleration moved issues of inclusion, gender equity, social justice, wellness, mental health, resilience, emotional intelligence and what it means to be an essential worker center stage for organizations large and small. Alone, any one of these could represent a force majeure for employers and workers alike. Unfortunately, for millions it was indeed. The collective impact of the 2020 experience will have a profound effect on how, when, where, and in what context we work, and ultimately, on who will thrive in the future of work throughout this decade.

My story is one of shifts, pivots, reinvention, continuous learning, fierce curiosity, and a relentless drive to rise above, live and work with impact and thrive on my terms. My story is also about daring to be audaciously bold as I fulfill my life's work with purpose and intention by empowering others to thrive on their terms as we move through the most crucial decade of work in our lifetimes.

The Future of Work Will Be a Force Majeure for Most

Workforce futurists, experts, and leading global research firms typically refer to the future of work as the period between 2020 and 2030. During this period, it is projected that organizations will experience significant technological disruption driven by the influence of Industry 4.0. First, let's unpack Industry 4.0. Industry 4.0 builds on Industry 3.0, which was all about the internet, computers, and automation. Comparatively, Industries 1.0, and 2.0 introduced steam, electricity, and mass production. However, unlike preceding industries, Industry

4.0 is all about hyper-connectivity, the Internet of Things, big data, predictive analytics, and futuristic technologies like AI, machine learning, deep learning, blockchain, 3D printing, computer vision, drones, and mixed reality, to name a few. It is also about an organization's ability to use and combine these technologies in extraordinarily novel ways that impact how we live, work, and play. So, simply put, the future of work is influenced by the availability of these technologies that subsequently enable organizations to combine data, technology, connected intelligence, and people in game-changing ways. Leveraging these technologies facilitates the digital transformation of organizations. Digital transformation is an iterative and innovative process that pumps blood through the veins of an organization and is actualized across culture, experiences, processes and the development of new products and services. As an example, in the future of work, organizations leverage these technologies to solve new problems, increase efficiency and accuracy, reduce costs, drive performance and engagement, humanize worker experiences, create immersive customer experiences, enter new markets and reconceptualize jobs in ways that were inconceivable in the past.

Let's take a look at a few examples. To shape purchase behavior, deliver a personalized customer experience and increase sales revenue, several fast-food restaurants use facial recognition to predict orders, make recommendations based on age, sentiment, and gender and identify preferences for future purchases. In the recruitment and selection space, to reduce the time and cost associated with hiring, increase candidate pools, improve the caliber of candidates, and assess cultural fit, many organizations use AI-powered neuroscience assessments and AI video interviewing platforms. These platforms rank candidates not only on answer quality, but also on facial, voice, and psychometric analysis outcomes.

In the learning and development space, many organizations

combine mixed reality and simulations to train workers on how to respond to theft, natural disasters, and even terror attacks to reduce psychological trauma, loss, and other risks. To deliver customer experiences and deepen emotional resonance, brands often combine AI with virtual reality and gamification to provide immersive experiences for customers to deeply engage with products before buying. In higher education, many universities use blockchain technology to log, track, manage, and verify academic credentials to deliver a more streamlined experience for students during the admissions process. These are just a few examples of how AI can transform organizational strategy, operations, products, services, and experiences.

Although we are in the infancy phases of both AI and the future of work, remember, the future of work is now, not tomorrow and it is advancing rapidly. As such, thousands of companies today provide AI-based solutions for virtually every industry and function to support and leverage digital transformation strategies. Whether predictive analytics, business intelligence, data science platforms, biometric analysis, natural language processing, data visualization, back-office automation, mixed reality, machine learning, or deep learning, many organizations use these technologies to competitively shapeshift business, customer and even people strategies. So, if we take a deeper dive into this, it is clear that as the future of work continues to evolve, a considerable number of tasks associated with most jobs will be replaced by AI technologies. It also means that most workers will work alongside many of these technologies, algorithms, bots, and robots to deliver higher-level value aligned with organizational strategy. The entire employee experience will be transformed. This transformation will impact all aspects of people strategy from recruitment to development, performance, engagement, well-being, inclusion, and retention.

Ironically, despite the rapid pace of AI adoption, a recent survey by Deloitte Insights, revealed that only one-fifth of executives believed that their workforce, including leaders, possessed the complex skills needed to succeed in the future of work. More troubling is that a 2019 IBM Research Insights report revealed that more than 120 million workers across the twelve largest economies in the world would need to be retrained by 2021. What is clear, is that most workers have not kept up with shifting work trends and changes in the workplace. These statistics point to why the future of work will be a force majeure for most. Remember, experts believed that COVID-19 accelerated the future of work by nearly a decade. Keep in mind, that these insights by Deloitte and IBM, were released before the pandemic.

As you remember, due to the pandemic, business for most industries came to a screeching halt. While virtually all industries were negatively impacted, several such as hospitality, restaurants, travel, entertainment, fitness, beauty, and retail bore the brunt of the pain. We later learned that women, too, bore the brunt of the impact of the pandemic. Most states enacted stay-at-home orders, social distancing was mandated, and consumer spending plummeted. To ensure business continuity, employers transitioned vast amounts of the workforce to remote work, transfigured operations, shifted business strategies, and created new revenue streams. During this time, employers also ramped up investment and implementation of AI systems that, pre-COVID, were scheduled as far out as 2025. Organizations, that were already behind in digital and structural transformation, and lacked meaningful competitive advantage, suffered gravely, and COVID-19 proved to be their force majeure. The rapid progression of the future of work between now and 2030 will be a force majeure for organizations unable to keep pace with advancing digital technologies and processes, shifting consumer preferences and the demands of the competitive landscape.

As we move into what is called the post-COVID era, it is projected that substantial investment in AI systems will occur across all corners of the enterprise for the foreseeable future to drive resilience, agility, revenue, and innovation. In fact, McKinsey & Company referred to the post-COVID era as the "great un-freezing" in which organizations move from surviving to thriving.

As organizations continue the process of un-freezing" and transition into the post-pandemic thriving stage, the impact on workers will be swift and deep. In 2020, between March and May, 40 million jobs were lost in the United States due to COVID-19. It is estimated that nearly 40% of the job losses will be permanent – despite the positive impact of the "great un-freezing". Roles from the C-suite to the mailroom and everything in between will be reimagined. Work will be more remote, hybrid, on-demand, fluid, mobile, data-driven and augmented by AI. As the employment terrain shifts, we will need fewer accounting, medical coding, human resource, marketing, supply chain, retail, distribution, engineering, energy, healthcare, higher education, and manufacturing professionals. I could go on, but I know you get the point. The competitive environment will BE ABSOLUTELY FIERCE. Those who lack the background, expertise, right combination of skills, knowledge, and experiences and a high level of emotional intelligence will be left behind. Undeniably, the COVID-accelerated future of work is a force majeure in the making for most organizations and people.

WHAT YOU NEED TO DO

Let me be clear, this does not mean that you must become a data scientist, systems engineer, or programmer. What this does mean, however, is that just as you have a fundamental understanding of how Alexa, Siri, Google Assistant, Instacart, and social media platforms work, you must have a fundamental understanding of what AI is and is not, and how it is used to solve business problems, improve processes, experiences and replace tasks. Most importantly, you must understand the impact on the purpose, design and reimagination of the job you have today and those you will have in the future.

I want you to fully accept that the future of work is materializing at this very moment before your eyes and that the work you do or plan to do will be impacted and augmented in some way by AI regardless of industry, role, or position. I want you to recognize that if the unfolding of the future of work compounded by COVID-19, deep recessionary economic conditions, protests, and civil and political unrest can upend industries, shutter iconic brands, and fundamentally transform consumer behavior, then you, too, can be impacted and therefore must transform. Your transformation will require insights, guidance, reflection, planning, and action. I will guide you through this process in each chapter. When you finish the book, you will have a multifaceted plan to put into action. I call it the Thrive Plan, because it is what you must unapologetically focus on if you plan to thrive in the future. Just as in the figure below, I want you to be able to stare the future of work squarely in the face as if you already own it so that you will be resilient, relevant, bold, and thrive on your terms!

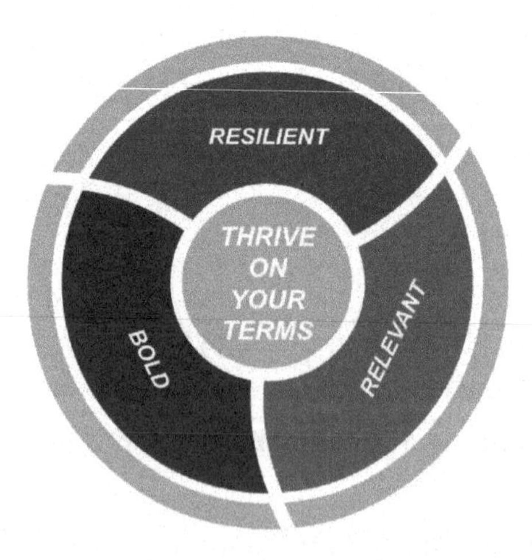

Figure 1. Framework for Thriving on Your Terms in the Future of Work

HOW YOU GET THERE

To begin the process of developing your plan to ensure that the unfolding of the future of work will not be your force majeure, start here:

- **Develop** the right mindset – resilient, flexible, adaptive, curious, and creative
- **Remember** your pandemic experience – what you learned, and how you grew
- **Find** your superpower – you will need it
- **Lean** into the future – it is coming whether you face it or not, master reinventing
- **Investigate** how your industry, organization, specialization, and role will be transformed by 2030
- **Create** a vision of what you want to do, who you want to be in the future of work
- **Identify** and eliminate gaps in education, knowledge, and skills
- **Develop** your plan, build your network, execute, thrive on your terms!

Be bold and audacious enough to know that you will work and thrive on your terms!

Dr. Terri Horton
FUTURIST

PERSONAL REFLECTION

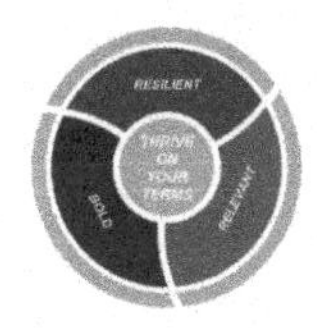

The purpose of this reflection is to uncover any angst or trepidation you might have about the future of work, address how you might be disrupted, and to identify the strengths and superpowers you possess that will propel you through the shifts and pivots needed to thrive on your terms.

1. What three things excite you the most about the future of work?
2. What intimidates you the most about the future of work?
3. How did the COVID-19 pandemic alter your perceptions or expectations about how the future of work will unfold by 2030?
4. Are you prepared to shift, pivot, and adapt? What are you willing to do?
5. What is the one action you can take to ensure that the future of work is not your force majeure?

YOUR THRIVE PLAN

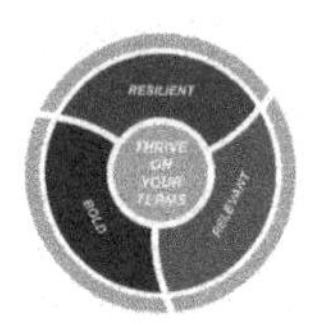

Part 1 “Stare the Future of Work Squarely in the Face”

You will develop a Thrive Plan for each chapter. For your first plan, you will identify three goals related to leveling up your understanding of what the future of work means to you, how you may be affected and how you want to show up in the future of work. Identify key actions, desired results, resources, skills, knowledge or training, networking or partnerships required and a relevant timeline. Most importantly, identify how this goal and related actions get you closer to owning the future of work on your terms!

THRIVE PLAN

GOAL

GOAL & TIMELINE

RESOURCES

ACCOUNTABILITY PARTNER

DESIRED OUTCOMES & SUCCESS MEASUREMENTS

HOW GOAL SUPPORTS THRIVING

THRIVE PLAN

GOAL

GOAL & TIMELINE

RESOURCES

ACCOUNTABILITY PARTNER

DESIRED OUTCOMES & SUCCESS MEASUREMENTS

HOW GOAL SUPPORTS THRIVING

THRIVE PLAN

GOAL

GOAL & TIMELINE

RESOURCES

ACCOUNTABILITY PARTNER

DESIRED OUTCOMES & SUCCESS MEASUREMENTS

HOW GOAL SUPPORTS THRIVING

THRIVE PLAN NOTES

PART 1
"STARE THE FUTURE OF WORK SQUARELY IN THE FACE"

2

THE COVID-ALTERED FUTURE OF WORK

The Path Forward 2020–2030

"If you can't fly then run, if you can't run then walk, if you can't walk then crawl, but whatever you do you have to keep moving forward."

—Martin Luther King Jr.—

How I Found My Path Forward

As I rang in the new year at midnight in 2019, I was thrilled to begin the new decade. On the first day of the new year, I opened my eyes to the promise of 2020. As a futurist, I knew the period between 2020 and 2030 would be one of the most dynamic and revolutionary decades of our lifetime due to how AI and automation would change everything. I was excited and ready! After all, my business was thriving. I was selected to deliver a keynote on digital literacy at Oxford University in the United Kingdom. I was negotiating with a new client in Australia to provide artificial intelligence business strategy training for executives. I was also selected to give my first TEDx talk and was in the process of making travel plans for a trip to China in late 2020. It was only January and I had contracts underway for nearly $100K in business for 2020. I remember meeting a colleague for lunch to catch up and discuss what we envisioned for 2020. We concluded that if our businesses continued to thrive at the current pace, 2020 would be phenomenal! Our excitement about 2020 was palatable. It was as if we were kids at our birthday party waiting to tear off the wrapping paper and dive into the sea of toys on our wish lists. Clearly, without trepidation, we could not wait for 2020 to deliver on its promise. Little did we know, however, that a global pandemic and economic crisis were looming. Little did we know that the coronavirus would infect and kill hundreds of thousands, shut down countries, industries, and nearly businesses of all stripes. Little did we know that social distancing would metamorphize the workplace, consumer behavior and that few would emerge unscathed personally or professionally.

In February, the US declared COVID-19 a public health emergency. It was then that what I built, developed, and was ready to receive as the promise of 2020 began to disintegrate – just as we learned later how soap, hand sanitizer, and Lysol would disintegrate the virus itself. During February, March, and April, I was caught in an endless virulent web of client cancelations. COVID-19 was in the truest sense a contractual force majeure. It was devastating and impacted every aspect of my business. It was overwhelming, chaotic, and sadly disappointing, to say the least. I canceled international trips, checked the pulse of clients and partners, and stabilized the business that remained. I also consumed as much strategic business, economic, and pandemic data, and insights as possible so that I could begin to rationalize the path forward. It was exhausting.

For a month, I felt like I was drowning. For the first time in decades, the intrepid futurist was shaken by the uncertainty of the future. At times, the cacophony of it all was deafening as I searched for the new next and concurrently guided clients, colleagues, students, and family through the opacity of the time. However, I knew that if I kept moving, kept learning, kept exploring, and reimagining the path forward, I would find new green shoots, meaning, and context for the next new normal. I also knew that much of how we live, consumed data, shopped, celebrated, and ultimately worked would never return to pre-COVID-19 norms. So, I leaned into the new next.

While it was challenging, focusing on the path forward enabled me to see and shift to several new strategic opportunities that emerged during the historic global confluence of the pandemic, depression-era economic conditions, and the burgeoning social justice movement. While some of my work as a futurist and university lecturer remained unscathed, I expanded my expertise to provide strategies to solve for the impact of the unprecedented confluence of challenges faced by organizations and people. This approach filled the gaps and gave flight to COVID-related business and people strategy consulting, coaching, training, and speaking contracts. This concentrated focus on the path forward also paved the runway for a smooth landing to provide global management consultancies in the US, Europe, Asia, and Africa with strategic insights on the new next. As record unemployment, layoffs, and transitions surged driving professionals to upskill and level-up, I pivoted and looked to leverage my expertise in non-traditional higher education programs. As a result, I secured a contract as a facilitator with an Ivy League university. It was exhausting. At times, I felt like an air traffic controller staring at a chaotic screen trying to direct the safe landing of thousands of planes suspended in the sky...but I persisted.

In the end, I reframed the problem and flipped what could have been a force majeure for my business. Focusing on the path forward, I did not allow the problem to metastasize. I concentrated on how I could deliver value and provide solutions. I refused to let the impact of

COVID-19, a real global force majeure no less, virulently attack and destroy my purpose, vision, and goals for the foundational year of the new decade. It was not easy though. There were a lot of sleepless nights and lots of prayer. I questioned everything and, at times, had dips in confidence. It was an iterative process, requiring constant assessment and management of risk grounded in value, growth, and thriving on the path forward. It was not about trying to survive and ultimately thrive by totally recreating the pre-COVID-19 model, but rather by reimagining and preparing for new lanes and runways. It was about planning and evaluating new scenarios and being resilient. It was about objectively and realistically evaluating the impact of the crisis and catalyzing change in response to the new tsunami of complexity and uncertainty while focusing on a new and different future. As a futurist, the path is always forward even if fog clouds the view.

The Path Forward

It is important to remember that the path forward is just that... forward. As I discussed in the first chapter of this book, COVID-19 accelerated the unfolding of the future of work by nearly ten years. It accelerated the move to telehealth in healthcare, the move to remote learning from K-12 to colleges and universities, the explosive growth in the home fitness space, e-commerce, and fast-forwarded the touch-less economy. So, without fully rationalizing how fundamentally the world and business changed due to the pandemic and what that means to you, your path forward will be compromised. It will be paved with paradigms, business strategies, and career models that will keep you anchored in the past and deploying strategies that neither fully advance your journey nor enable you to experience the potential that blooms beneath uncertainty and awaits you in the future.

Leading global consulting firms such as McKinsey, Deloitte, Kantar, and Accenture published insights and guidance for organizations in the first half of 2020 with the strategic focus of not returning to the old but rather capitalizing on what was learned and pivoting forward in the next normal. The collective guidance followed a common theme centered on resilience, resetting, reskilling, reinventing, and ultimately returning to the market with a relentless focus not on surviving but rather thriving on the path forward.

There are countless examples of companies that responded to the impact of the pandemic and economic crisis by resetting, reinventing, and preparing to thrive in an evolving and uncertain future. In response to the pandemic induced downturns in international, business, and domestic travel, and the increase in remote work, many luxury hotels across the globe rented out rooms as office space to not only respond to professionals social distancing and work-life balance demands but also to create new subscription model revenue streams for the future. Online streaming services created pandemic-centric programming, and parking lots became pop-up drive-in movie experiences. An animal sanctuary in California, impacted by stay-at-home orders, lost revenue generated from visitors. So, the owners pivoted to a new model, which was incredibly creative. They created a service to combat video meeting fatigue. Companies could rent a variety of farm animals from goats to llamas to create virtual interactions with meeting participants and virtual tours of the sanctuary. The new model garnered the sanctuary hundreds of new clients, and they expanded the model to virtual happy hours and an intriguing version of "bring your child to work day" for remote workers. I must admit this is one of my favorite examples. I suspect this model will live on long after the pandemic ends.

Think about all the creativity and innovation that emerged in response to the COVID-19 economy. Think about all the people who became makers of designer face masks, shields and helmets, and COVID-19 themed apparel to inspire hope and resilience. Think about people who were laid off, furloughed, or took advantage of the time regained from commuting to repurpose and monetize their expertise. Stylists and make-up artists refocused their expertise to create home beauty kits for those of us traumatized by the thought of coloring our own hair or doing our own facials, manicures, pedicures, and waxing. College counselors launched platforms and masterclasses to provide students longing for the campus experience yet relegated to online learning with mentoring, career guidance, and speed networking sessions. Data scientists responding to the increased use of video interviews by employers driven by social distancing, taught job seekers how to improve their odds of being selected by recruiting algorithms. Personal trainers and yoga instructors launched online subscription-based sessions while laid-off marketers levied their expertise to launch business development services. Resilience, resetting, reskilling, and reinventing is arduous, but companies and ordinary people did it to survive and set the stage for thriving on the other side.

You can do the same on your terms and find your path forward by embracing challenges and new possibilities so that you can thrive in one of the most consequential decades of our lifetimes! It will be a challenge, but you are more resilient and adaptive than you realize. Your journey through this book will be focused on resilience, relevancy, boldness, and thriving! So, in the spirit of Dr. King, even if you need to crawl towards the path forward – crawl until you can walk. If you can walk to the path forward – walk until you can run. If you can run to the path forward – take off. My goal is to help you fly. Onward!

3

BE EMOTIONALLY INTELLIGENT AND RESILIENT

The Post-COVID-19 Power Currencies

"The bamboo that bends is stronger than the oak that resists."

—Japanese Proverb—

Resilience Does Not Come Easy

The year before the pandemic, I was selected to write a chapter for a book about women and courage. I was delighted to be one of several female co-authors, all of whom were successful and accomplished, sharing stories and experiences to inspire others. As I began to write, I had an epiphany, and it was profound. I realized that, from an early age, I fundamentally understood the intersectionality of resilience and courage, even if I could not explain it. The epiphany led me back to one of my earliest memories and experiences in leveraging them like superpowers to recover and audaciously keep moving forward.

I started first grade at four years old. My parents enrolled me in a prep school in Hollywood. The children of several Hollywood notables attended the school, as did many child actors. From time to time, I recognized the faces of children whom I regularly watched on television. I remember my first day as if it were yesterday. I remember walking down the long hallway with the shiny black marble floor; everyone and everything seemed so big. I was dwarfed by the building, the children and adults swiftly moving through the hallways. As I continued down the hall holding my mother's hand and approached the doorway of my classroom, my mother hugged me and gave me her signature look, indicating that everything would be just fine. My teacher warmly greeted me, but I was afraid, and I cried. I clung to her dress as she walked me to the front of the room and introduced me to the rest of the class.

At the time, I was an only child, spent most of my time around adults, and was frightened by the six and seven-year-old first graders staring back at me, none of whom, by the way, looked anything like me.

Although I was a gifted child and could read at a first-grade level at four years old, I was afraid and cried every day for the first few weeks. While the work seemed easy, facing my first-grade peers, and figuring out where I fit in was the challenge. As time progressed, I found the courage to stop the tears and just own it. I learned to walk down the shiny black marble hallway of the prep school every day with my perfectly coifed ponytails, put one black patent leather shoe in front of the other, sit in the front of the class and learn on my four-year-old terms. At four years old, I found a way to harness the power of resilience. Of course, I could not explain or fully comprehend it conceptually. I just knew that I had to keep going and that when I earned it, I belonged anywhere that I chose. That is my first memory of resilience. At four years old, unbeknownst to me, throughout my career, I would walk down many historical corporate, and institutional shiny marble hallways, often be the first, defy stereotypes and profoundly prove my right to move into spaces I could not have imagined and most importantly, that resilience would be one of my greatest strengths.

One of my favorite quotes on resilience is by Nelson Mandela. He said, "Don't judge me by my success; judge me by how many times I fell and got back up." This quote resonates deeply with me on several levels. In my twenties and early thirties, when I was beginning my career in media, I did not have the degrees and credentials that I have today. In fact, I did not have any of them. I graduated from high school with a 4.0 GPA and received a full college scholarship. While that was a fantastic accomplishment, unfortunately, I became bored and quit after three years. And let me tell you, after returning to college fifteen years later and paying out of pocket, that decision ranks nearly at the top of my life regrets list. But I digress. As I forged my career, the fact that I did not have a college degree was a heavy weight to bear, and along the way, I encountered colleagues brash enough to remind me. But what I did know was that I was smart, was resilient, and had grit. So, I carried the weight. It got heavier at times as I advanced and imposter syndrome kicked in, but I carried the weight, nevertheless. Not only did I need resilience to keep moving forward in my career without a degree, but I especially needed it when I returned to college to complete my degree. Although I had dropped out fifteen years before, the stakes were higher. I was afraid that I might not be able to finish or fail for some reason.

At the time, I could not have imagined that finding a way to conquer the fear of returning would ignite the desire to complete two master's degrees and, years later, a doctorate. To move forward, I had to acknowledge that returning to college conjured emotions of fear and worthiness. If I did not self-regulate and manage my emotions, that same fear of failure would negatively impact the motivation and resilience I needed to complete my academic journey.

The funny thing about resilience is that most of us are more resilient than we believe and that every fear we conquer, every accomplishment, and every box we check builds up a reservoir of resilience that we can tap into at any time. However, sometimes we need a nudge or reminder along the way to tap into the power of our emotional intelligence. The year 2020, with all its chaos, challenges, and pain triggered the need for a nudge, a reminder, a symbol if you will, to remind us of our resilience and true grit in times of extreme uncertainty. I am pretty resilient, but in the first several weeks of the shutdown, as I searched to understand the current and future impact of the pandemic while looking for signals, signposts and meaning for what would be the new normal, I needed a nudge. So, I became more spiritual, sought answers from my ancestors through their writings and stories. I collaborated with colleagues and of course, sought the insights and guidance of my favorite auntie. You know the one, the auntie who has lived a remarkably successful life, adores you, seems to know everything and always gives it to you straight. Yes, that one! In a nutshell, she told me that 2020 would be a process, but that my foundation was sturdy, that I know who I am and where I want to go, and not even 2020 or a pandemic gets to mess with that! In 2020, my nudge came in the form of a four-pronged assault; it was spiritual, ancestral, relational, and dare I coin a new term, "aunt-factual". It worked!

Emotional intelligence impacts how we see and manage ourselves, how we interact with others and informs our approach to resilience. As a futurist, emotional intelligence and resilience lay the foundation for me to navigate the unknown, look for signals, engage in foresight and scenario planning, and thrive in uncertainty. Throughout my life, whether the four-year-old in a first-grade classroom, the adult learner returning to college, the media executive turned consultant in career 2.0, or the futurist in 2020, emotional intelligence and resilience have given me the wings I needed to fly.

Without a doubt, you will need resilience to thrive in the

momentous unfolding of the future of work. Along the way, you will need nudges, reminders, and in some cases coaching to find or reignite your inner fight. But, once you do, you will have the power to catalyze change and trade on the currencies of emotional intelligence and resilience so that you can experience your full potential in this decade.

COVID-19 Exposed Organizational Resilience

Resilience reveals how responsive and adaptive an organization is to change and disruption. However, to respond, adapt, and thrive amid change and disruption, an organization must have the capability to anticipate impending change and disruption. As we think about resilience in this context, the pandemic exposed the frailties of countries across the globe. It flipped industries upside down and pierced the vulnerable underbelly of organizations, revealing the secrets of both titans and aspirants. The year 2020 was a collective Black Swan event, and no one could have predicted the world would experience a deadly pandemic, social justice movement, political unrest, and economic tumult all at the same time. Most organizations were neither prepared for any of these singularly nor the collective impact to operational, people, reputational, or financial strategies. Moreover, most were unable to fathom that as the days, weeks and months went by, emotionally intelligent and resilient leaders would be in high demand to quell the angst of Boomer, Gen X, Millennial, and Gen Z employees suffering from "Zoom" fatigue, increased levels of anxiety and depression and decreased levels of engagement and productivity.

Most could not fathom the wave of women from executives to support staff, desperately balancing the weight of competing personal, familial, and professional priorities, while contemplating exiting the workforce. Most could not fathom the level of stress workers would experience while working remotely, feeling as if they were constantly "on." Most could not contemplate the deep level of vulnerability experienced by employees as they opened a digital window through the lens of video meeting platforms and exposed how they lived to colleagues and managers. Most could not fathom the level of emotional intelligence and empathy needed to help workers juggle homeschooling, conjure the resilience needed while teetering on the brink of financial ruin, or saying goodbye to loved ones who succumbed to the virus. Most could not fathom how emotionally intelligent leaders would need to extend corporate culture, collaboration, engagement, and community virtually, as workers concurrently experienced furloughs, salary reductions, and seemingly unending training in tandem with AI productivity metrics and analytics.

There are several reasons most organizations were unprepared, and experts will chronicle and debate the reasons, for decades to come. In my view, there are three core reasons most organizations were blindsided and struggled to deploy the level of resilience needed to get up from the shock, dust off, quickly ensure business continuity, and insulate operations, people, and customers. First, the risk management function in most organizations lacks the capability to fully assess and synthesize external and global risks, identify acute drivers of risk, and balance risk appetite with cross-functional collaboration, innovation, and growth. Therefore, full-scale scenario planning can be compromised. In this context, if most risk functions lacked the capability to fully assess risks to corporate strategy, continuity, innovation, and growth, how could they sound the alarm about the impending devastating effects of the pandemic and social and political unrest that would reverberate across economies, industries, and organizations?

The second reason is that most organizations were in the infancy stages of building out future of work strategies. This means that many organizations had aging business models, infrastructure and, people strategies and therefore, were not positioned to optimize technology as a means of driving future-focused organizational redesign. Conversely, future-focused organizations are buckled up and positioned to respond to impending disruption. They can brazenly shift culture, business, people, and customer strategies, in ways and at a pace incomprehensible to stagnant legacy organizations and others that acutely lag in driving change and agility. A 2020 Gartner report on HR priorities emphasized the critical importance of building operational excellence and resilience into future of work and digital transformation strategies to offset disruption and drive growth and innovation through 2023.

Let's unpack this in a highly relatable context. Think about the industries that were impacted by COVID-19. Industries most negatively impacted included:

- Retail
- Real Estate
- Energy
- Restaurants
- Travel and hospitality
- Fitness and beauty
- Gaming
- Education
- Entertainment
- Healthcare
- Insurance

Stop for a moment and think of the major brands that filed for bankruptcy in 2020 due to shifts in consumer preferences and behavior combined with reduced spending. According to Forbes near the end of 2020, some of the brands that filed for bankruptcy as a result of COVID-19 included:

- Century 21 Department Stores
- Whiting Petroleum
- Lord & Taylor
- Garden Fresh Restaurants
- Guitar Center

- Dean and Deluca
- Trans States Airlines
- Sizzler USA
- Stein Mart
- California Pizza Kitchen
- Tailored Brands
- Brooks Brothers
- Sur La Table
- Chesapeake Energy
- CEC Entertainment
- Hertz
- 24 Hour Fitness
- Cirque du Soleil
- Apex Parks
- CMX Cinemas
- JC Penney
- Diamond Offshore Drilling
- Gold's Gym
- Neiman Marcus
- Pier 1 Imports

Think about how many of your favorite local small businesses, restaurants, spas, hair salons, and shoe repair shops have closed and may not reopen because of the impact of COVID-19. Think about how many companies, due to stay-at-home orders, were not prepared to effectively deploy a remote workforce with the right technology, capable of sustaining worker and customer experience or mitigating risks to brand reputation, processes, revenue, and cybersecurity. These examples reinforce the absolute importance of building resilience and fortifying resilience as a strategy so that organizations are prepared for and can restructure business models and people strategies with agility when faced with unforeseen and unplanned disruptions. Yes, resilience is the power currency not only for people but also for organizations. It will further define the relevancy of brands in the future.

The third reason is that many organizations did not have enough future-focused leaders in place with the foresight, multifunctional expertise, digital, analytic, AI or emotional intelligence needed to advance required change, redesign the organizations of the future, or humanize the worker experience, in response to the pandemic. A 2020

Deloitte Insights report revealed that COVID-19 served as a tool to refine resilient leadership. Think of the shrapnel the pandemic embedded in the underbelly of exposed organizations as leaders without the right strategies and competencies scurried to sustain engagement, productivity, and performance, discover new revenue streams, attend to the wounds of remote workers, disrupted vendors, partners, and disenchanted customers, without the foresight and emotional intelligence needed to properly mitigate the impact of the wounds. Conversely, many organizations led by emotionally intelligent and resilient leaders were able to respond, shift, galvanize employees and move through the chaos of 2020 with solid business resilience strategies and are poised to thrive as they redesign and lead organizations through the decade.

WHAT YOU NEED TO DO

Economists predict that the negative economic impact of COVID-19 and record-high levels of unemployment in the United States will linger for years and possibly extend beyond the middle of this decade. We know that the pandemic accelerated enterprise adoption of AI systems and platforms, which will require rapid and frequent reskilling, amend our relationship with work, and reshape our perspectives on careers. However, there is a reason for optimism. But you will need the right mindset to be optimistic and take advantage of opportunities that emerge and allow you to thrive.

Some of the opportunities will be augmentations of the work you do today. Others will fall outside of the scope of what you deem possible today. At the same time, others will emerge in entirely different sectors, categories, and roles beyond your current expertise and interest. Unsurprisingly, many of the opportunities you will discover, do not exist today, but are on the horizon for tomorrow. As a point of reference, use my example. I started my career in the media industry, and years later became a workforce futurist. I reinvented in a totally different industry and category, with a new set of combined expertise and skills providing solutions for clients to problems that did not exist ten years prior. You can do the same.

You will need to use emotional intelligence and resilience to train yourself to see what is unseen to most, what has been amplified by COVID-19, and what emerges for you in between the disruption and reimagination of how we work, live, and play and what that means to organizations, society, and people. You will need resilience as you identify opportunities to combine your expertise and skills in novel ways to reinvent or create a new path. You will also need emotional intelligence and resilience to adapt and develop strategies that combine several frameworks and models to identify new opportunities and spaces as the future of work continues to unfold. For example, I often combine psychology, strategy, innovation, change and AI implementation models and frameworks with future of work foresight and scenario planning to evaluate the impact of AI and identify emerging needs and demands for humanizing worker experience. In doing so, I can identify workers' emerging needs and help organizations develop strategies that support meaningful work, balance, development, inclusion, and responsible data practices, which underpin worker experience, engagement, and performance. I do this focused on the end game of developing strategies that enable workers to be resilient, relevant, bold, and thrive.

Emotional intelligence and resilience will enable you to see new possibilities and have the grit to stay the course until you achieve what you want in this decade. However, you will need to work at growing your emotional intelligence and practice building and maintaining a high level of resilience to sustain the focus and momentum you will need. The EQi-2.0 model is my go-to model for emotional intelligence. Let's walk through the model in the context of the future of work. The model demonstrates that self-awareness and self-regard are needed to understand, express, and assert yourself, build relationships, and self-actualize. In doing so, you will make better decisions and be able to assess shifting demands and environments realistically and objectively in the future. You will need flexibility and self-regulation to respond to the rapid, radical change and disruption of the decade to be adaptable, manage stress, reduce impulsivity, and be optimistic. All of this will support your well-being, happiness, ability to be resilient and ultimately thrive as you stake your claim in this decade on your terms.

HOW YOU GET THERE

To begin the process of developing your plan to become more emotionally intelligent and resilient start here:

- **Get** an emotional intelligence assessment
- **Consider** EQ and resilience coaching
- **Get** comfortable with uncertainty and transitions
- **Remind** yourself of times that you managed through change, uncertainty, overcame a setback, or catalyzed creativity, innovation, and growth
- **Develop** a daily self-care or recharging practice

Be so resilient that you walk into the future certain of your ability to own it!

Dr. Terri Horton
FUTURIST

PERSONAL REFLECTION

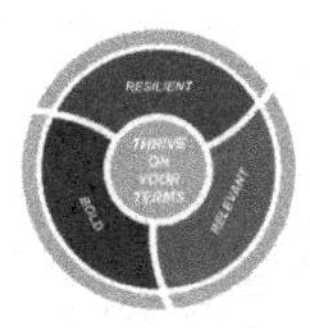

The purpose of this reflection is to uncover your strengths and opportunities for development related to your emotional intelligence and resilience.

1. The four components of emotional intelligence are self-awareness, self-management (resilience), social awareness, and relationship management.

   Which components of emotional intelligence are your greatest strengths, and how will these strengths support your journey through the disruption and the discovery of new opportunities in the future of work?

2. Which areas of emotional intelligence do you need to develop? How will failure to develop them impact your journey through the future of work?

3. Resilience is the ability to bounce back after a setback, disappointment, or failure and return stronger. How do you deal with setbacks, disappointment, and failure? Are you easily defeated, or do you bounce back?

4. Does your resilience enable you to take risks, adapt to change, and handle volatility, uncertainty, complexity, and ambiguity? Why or why not?

5. How might your weaknesses in emotional intelligence and resilience interfere with your ability to realistically take the proper actions to thrive on your terms?

YOUR THRIVE PLAN

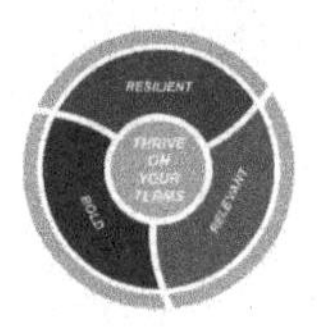

Part 2 "Emotional Intelligence and Resilience Are My Power Currencies"

For the second part of your plan, you will identify three goals and actions related to leveling up your emotional intelligence, resilience, and leveraging them as the power currencies that will enable you to move forward, be more self-aware, bounce back, shift and pivot in the future of work. Identify three goals, key actions, desired results, resources, skills, knowledge or training, networking or partnerships required, an accountability partner, and a relevant timeline. Most importantly, identify how each goal and related actions get you closer to owning the future of work on your terms!

THRIVE PLAN

GOAL

GOAL & TIMELINE

RESOURCES

ACCOUNTABILITY PARTNER

DESIRED OUTCOMES & SUCCESS MEASUREMENTS

HOW GOAL SUPPORTS THRIVING

THRIVE PLAN

GOAL

GOAL & TIMELINE

RESOURCES

ACCOUNTABILITY PARTNER

DESIRED OUTCOMES & SUCCESS MEASUREMENTS

HOW GOAL SUPPORTS THRIVING

THRIVE PLAN

GOAL

GOAL & TIMELINE

RESOURCES

ACCOUNTABILITY PARTNER

DESIRED OUTCOMES & SUCCESS MEASUREMENTS

HOW GOAL SUPPORTS THRIVING

THRIVE PLAN NOTES

PART 2
"EMOTIONAL INTELLIGENCE & RESILIENCE ARE MY POWER CURRENCIES"

4

BE HYPER-RELEVANT

Think, Act, Perform Like a Futurist and Collect Your Receipts

"The most reliable way to predict the future is to create it."

—ANONYMOUS—

So, You Think You're Relevant

The truth of the matter is that you are probably not as relevant as you tell yourself you are. Being relevant is relative, right? If we view relevancy through the lens of relativity, therein lies the challenge. Often, we view our relevancy in real time, through our lens, in our context and with our perceptions and perspectives. Unpack this with me. The Cambridge Dictionary defines relevant as "related to a subject or something that is happening or being discussed." Conversely, antonyms for the word relevant include insignificant, trivial, valueless, unimportant, and unsuitable. Naturally, as professionals and humans for that matter, the thought of being insignificant, or unsuitable is incredibly painful, undesirable, and unsustainable. Therefore, most of us fight against insignificance and work hard at developing and sustaining relevancy. For some of us, irrelevancy is one of our greatest fears.

The problem is most people seek and develop relevancy for the moment. Don't take the word moment literally. In this context, think of a moment as one to two years. If you are familiar with the term the "half-life of skills," you can get a deeper sense of where I am going with this point. The half-life of skills refers to the amount of time it takes from acquiring a skill until that skill is outdated or no longer relevant. The half-life of skills two decades ago was about five years. It was projected that by 2020 the half-life of skills would be two years, and roughly 30% of the skills we possess would be irrelevant, unsuitable, and insignificant. Need I remind you, this prediction was made long before the 2020 COVID-19 pandemic? This means that what you may believe are the receipts to prove your relevancy may not be sustainable. You need sustainable receipts. You need to be uber-adaptable to collect receipts that will sustain your brand over time. The ultimate receipt is a rock-solid future-proofed personal brand.

As you remember, COVID-19 accelerated the unfolding of the future of work by nearly a decade. So, the best estimates are that many of the skills we believe ground us in relevancy today are becoming more and more irrelevant as you read this very chapter. As we moved through the pandemic wearing face masks to protect us from spreading and contracting the virus, in a way, the pandemic stripped off the mask of presumed relevancy for many who believed they were relevant only to discover how many of their skills, strategies, and paradigms were insignificant and unsuitable. In many cases, they found themselves among the tens of millions of workers laid off or furloughed due to the impact of the pandemic. I can think of several colleagues who believed their industry, work and role were impermeable to the pandemic-fueled shockwaves that rolled through 2020. They had worked in the same industries in the same senior roles with the same skills and marginally future-proofed brands for decades and were certain that they were skilled-up enough and did not really need a Plan B.

By the end of 2020, nearly half of these colleagues had been furloughed, forced to accept reduced salaries, or completely displaced with no clear path forward. What we learned in the year of the pandemic was that nearly 40% of the layoffs, furloughs and salary reductions would be permanent. Not only did most of those affected lack the relevant skills to return to the workplace, but the majority were also oblivious to the fact that the use of recruitment AI systems and platforms for ranking, assessing, interviewing, and selecting candidates had accelerated due to pandemic related stay-at-home orders, and remote work. They were not prepared for the algorithms, natural language processing, biometric and psychometric analysis embedded in video interview platforms. They were not prepared for the neuroscience-based assessments used to select candidates with the right combinations of cross-functional, complex-problem solving, and emotional intelligence skills, the right cultural fit, and propensity for engagement. Think of the entrepreneurs forced during the pandemic to quickly shift direction, create new business and revenue models, new products and services, and leverage technology, data, and basic AI platforms. How many do you remember, who were unable to shift because they lacked the right, relevant combination of skills, acumen, infrastructure, e-commerce platforms, or ability to pivot through the thick, murky uncertainty and ambiguity that 2020 delivered? They simply were not ready! Shifts in markets, in competition, technology, consumer preferences and behaviors, drive shifts in business strategy. Shifts in business strategy drive shifts in people strategies. Shifts in people strategies drive shifts in skill requirements. Shifts in skill requirements drive irrelevancy. If you are not ready with the right combinations of skills and experience you will be poised for a force majeure.

Let's talk about mindset. To be relevant, you need a growth

mindset: a mindset fixated on embracing change, continuous learning, development, growth, inspiration, creativity, imagination, and reinvention. Most importantly, you must be compelled by your growth mindset to see relevancy in the future of work through a new paradigm of hyper-relevancy. Your perspective on what it means to be relevant must change in the context of the future of work. You must be hyper-relevant, not just relevant. You must think about relevancy through the dimension of time and space. You must think of relevancy differently in breadth and scope. Now, I want you to think of relevancy as a continuum of successfully acquiring, balancing, positioning, and leveraging skills and experiences in the framework of three domains: the domains of the now, the new next and the future. You will develop and manage all three domains concurrently. This will enable you to develop a future-focused brand and a reputation based on your knowledge, expertise, influence, results, and ability to leverage your skills and talent in ways that enable you to stay AHEAD of the future and deliver phenomenal value.

The new paradigm is hyper-relevancy. Period. You are only truly relevant if you stay ahead of the future by five to seven years. You are relevant if you deliver a high level of value today, already have the skills needed to deliver value in the next two to three years, and if you use those skills as consequential foundations for the skills, jobs, and opportunities that emerge in the post-pandemic economy and the future of work.

Being hyper-relevant is how you collect sustainable receipts that prove you are in it to win it in the future of work on your terms. You will think, act, and perform like a futurist. I want you to be hyper-relevant, future-focused, future-proofed and have powerful receipts. It will not be easy. It will take a lot of work and, require a hell of a lot of resilience. But the brand you build and the receipts you collect will be worth it. Unlike a vaccine aimed at reducing the impact and the spread of COVID-19, there is only one symbolic "vaccine" for preventing irrelevancy: do the work and get the receipts. My goal is to lead you through the process of becoming hyper-relevant and collecting the right receipts that sustain your brand and enable you to thrive through 2030.

The New Business of Skills and Relevancy

According to the PWC 2020 Global CEO survey conducted on Upskilling in an Uncertain World, CEOs have prioritized upskilling as a key component of competitive advantage through 2030. However, according to the survey only 20% indicated that their upskilling programs were significantly reducing skills gaps and mismatches. Ironically, the survey also revealed that 41% feared that increased investments in talent and skill development would decrease retention. This is a mind-blowing dichotomy. However, let's unpack it. According to a World Economic Forum study on upskilling in the future of work, while it is impossible to calculate the actual cost for all companies, it is estimated that the cost of upskilling is about $25,000 per employee. So, understandably, the fear of decreased retention is squarely rooted in a logical demand for a long-term return on investment. Nonetheless, the dichotomy remains. The short view is a myopic view rooted in the fear of skilled-up employees departing to leverage newly acquired skills with future employers. The long view on the other hand, focuses on the impact of upskilling on organizational culture, reputation, engagement, productivity, and retention as an intentional approach to long-term growth.

So, let's talk about the elephant in the room, which is the overarching cost of mitigating skill gaps in the United States. In a 2019 report, the World Economic Forum estimated that the cost for the United

States to upskill 25% of its workforce displaced by automation would be $34 billion dollars. The WEF further estimated that employers alone would only be able to shoulder 14% of the cost. The remainder of the cost, the WEF argued, could be offset by government, societal and other business investments. This means that most of the heavy lifting for upskilling, may fall on the shoulders of workers who are not fortunate enough to work for employers that foot some or all of the cost.

What I see as added perplexing challenges for organizations is identifying the right approach for upskilling with a relevant future focus and identifying the right hybrid, digital, data, analytic, AI, and soft skill combinations to embed in upskilling programs. Furthermore, the challenges of striking the right partnerships, accessing forward-looking skills data, leveraging the right learning platforms, using AI and virtual reality to personalize learning, and including micro-credentialing in upskilling programs often are significant barriers to implementation and often marginally address the needs of workers. Creating immersive social, mobile macro and micro-learning events, and experiences in hybrid work environments will also be a challenge for many organizations.

Let's pause and look at the definition of upskilling. PWC defined upskilling as, "an organization's clear intent to develop its employees' capabilities and employability, and to advance and progress the knowledge, skills and attitudes required to enhance business and individual performance." If we shine a light on the part of the definition that speaks to the clear intent of developing employees' capabilities and employability, one can argue that upskilling should be not only about current relevancy, but also about future relevancy for the worker and the employer. To that end, investing in upskilling is a strategic investment in organizational resilience and sustainability. It is without question, therefore, that learning, and development will be the currencies that differentiate employer brands. However, until most organizations embrace upskilling and out-skilling, which prepares workers for new jobs and career paths with or without their current employer, as a strategic priority, workers will have to figure out what skilling up for the future means as well as bear the cost.

While most organizations still have some work to do, when it comes to comprehensive upskilling programs, there are several organizations that get it, are reinventing the meaning of employee development, and are prioritizing future-focused strategies. In fact, The LinkedIn Learning 5th Annual report on Workplace Learning, which surveyed over 1,200 learning and development professionals from around the world, revealed that the number one area of focus in 2021 would be upskilling and reskilling employees. Let's take a look at a few examples.

- Amazon will upskill 100,000 employees for jobs that will be in demand by 2025. Amazon has developed several programs aimed at increasing tech literacy to help fulfillment center workers move into tech jobs, expanding existing tech workers into machine learning roles and training and certifying workers in cloud computing.
- PWC will invest $3 billion dollars to upskill 275,000 employees by 2025. The company plans to develop digital training tools and work with global organizations to upskill workers throughout the world.
- JP Morgan Chase will invest over $600 million to upskill its workforce. Acknowledging that the future of work is about skills, the company will upskill underrepresented workers and those in low-skill jobs to prepare them for the tech jobs of the future.
- IBM deployed an AI strategy to identify future in-demand skills targeted at providing training for disadvantaged communities. The term "New Collar" jobs was coined by the CEO to describe IBM's

approach to recruiting non-traditional employees without degrees, upskilling them in data science and hiring them for current and emerging tech jobs.

- Mastercard is upskilling staff through an online learning platform that delivers personalized learning focused on AI and tech aligned with its current and future service offerings.

As we move deeper into the decade, while some industries will implement faster than others, the broader business community will embrace components of upskilling and deploy a variety of strategies aimed at providing workers with the right combination of skills for today and tomorrow. By 2025, it is projected that half of all workers in the United States will need to reskill. This prediction was made by the World Economic Forum a year before the pandemic. In the interim, if you work for an organization with a learning culture that provides opportunities for you to participate in reskilling and upskilling programs, SEIZE the opportunities. If your current organization does not invest in comprehensive future-focused learning and upskilling, staying in the long term may pose an unnecessary threat to your brand sustainability and growth as well as limit your ability to thrive.

WHAT YOU NEED TO DO

Think, act, and perform like a futurist. Period. My goal is to provide you with strategies that enable you to see the future more clearly and to use that knowledge and insight to develop plans and strategies that are relevant, allow you to stay ahead of the future, avoid a force majeure and therefore, create your future on your terms. Remember the quote at the beginning of the chapter is "The most reliable way to predict the future is to create it." You will use data and insights as part of your strategy to continuously hone your skills and extend the breadth and scope of your future-focused personal brand. While none of us can predict the future with 100% accuracy, thinking, acting, and performing like a futurist can mitigate some of the workforce uncertainty and ambiguity of this decade. You can position yourself to harvest the skills and experiences you need as hybrid skills take center stage, work becomes more fluid, and on-demand, the war for talent is amplified and new roles emerge.

Think, act, and perform like a futurist. Period. Analyze trends, look for signals and use strategic foresight to identify and understand how work is changing, factors or levers shaping the change, and the multiple indicators of what is to come to develop future scenarios. Now, this is a rather simplistic explanation of how to study the future and strategic foresight, of course, but you can make this work for you, and it can enable you to get a better grasp on what it means to be relevant and help in predicting and modeling the future you want. Just as global management consulting firms and institutions of higher learning use scenario planning in strategic foresight to position organizations to thrive in the future, you must do the same for your personal brand and future career.

Think, act, and perform like a futurist. Period. Identify and understand what skills you need now, what skills you will need two to three years out, and you will be able to predict what new roles and skills might emerge as we move through 2030. I am often asked, what skills will be in most demand between 2020 and 2030 regardless of industry or function. In my view, the most important skills you need are hybrid cross-functional skills, statistics, data analysis, analytics and visualization, data science, programming, AI fluency, emotional intelligence, complex problem-solving, analogous thinking, creativity, cross-cultural competency, and resilience. I want you to look at what skills were identified by the World Economic Forum as most in demand for 2025 across all professions. Take a look at the categories and the related skills.

The World Economic Forum Top 10 Skills of 2025 – Skill Categories

- Problem solving
- Self-management
- Working with people
- Technical use and development

The World Economic Forum Top 10 Skills of 2025

- Analytical thinking and innovation
- Active learning and learning strategies
- Complex problem solving
- Critical thinking and analysis
- Creativity, originality, and initiative
- Leadership and social influence
- Technology use, monitoring and control
- Technology design and programming
- Resilience, stress tolerance and flexibility
- Reasoning, problem-solving and ideation

In the same report, the World Economic Forum outlined the amount of time required to acquire and master skills across the four categories of problem-solving, self-management, working with people, and technical use and development. According to the report, it is estimated that it will take one to three months to acquire and master one skill related to people and culture, two to five months to acquire and master one skill in data, AI, and programming. It should be clear that your learning and skill acquisition strategy will be continuous, and you will need a comprehensive plan to become hyper-relevant, stay ahead of the future and align your expertise with emerging opportunities. You cannot afford to risk your future by getting behind.

While many employers orchestrate upskilling and reskilling through learning and development departments, I recommend you also work with a coach with expertise in learning, the intersectionality of the future of work, and in-demand and emerging skill requirements to align your upskilling and reskilling with your plan for who you want to be in the future of work and how you expect to thrive on your terms. Your plan for hyper-relevancy should be multifaceted.

The challenge that most professionals experience lies in understanding how all of the skill requirements intersect and play out in specific roles, how employers' value and assess these skills and competencies, when and how to prioritize and acquire them and how exactly to leverage these skills to future-proof their brand. For example, the value and power of these skills and how to prioritize and position them vary from the human resource manager to the finance, operations, marketing, sales, or IT manager. Yet, all need the same skills contextualized around their specific function and expertise, and all must be able to demonstrate competencies clearly.

I'll use an example from the human resources discipline to help you unpack and understand what I mean. When coaching human resource executives responsible for driving digital transformation and the redesign of people strategies, I emphasize the critical importance of prioritizing, acquiring, demonstrating, and leveraging the following skills and competencies:

- future of work strategies
- foresight and scenario planning
- workforce analytics
- digital transformation
- corporate business strategy
- complex problem solving
- cross-functional expertise
- risk management
- growth and innovation
- marketing and branding
- diversity, inclusion, belonging
- data privacy and ethics
- storytelling
- virtual reality
- project management
- cybersecurity
- data science
- data analysis and visualization
- programming
- AI fluency
- design thinking
- creativity
- cross-cultural
- cross-generational
- emotional intelligence

It's A LOT, I get it. Keep in mind, these skills are in addition to the complex combination of skills and competencies specific to human resources. As you juxtapose these skills with the role that human resource executives will play in designing organizations of the future, how could you not expect a human resource executive to possess these skills and competencies? Let's look at another example. As healthcare organizations become more efficient and deliver higher levels of patient care, technology and AI will drive the transformation of hospital operations. The future of healthcare, will be optimized by technologies like robotics, machine learning, computer vision, genomics, and wearable tech. As such, CXO's will need backgrounds in technology, as well as skills and competencies in data science, AI, and automation to lead hospital systems through the transformation.

Here's what I want you to understand. At the end of the day, you need to master the skills required NOW. Start acquiring the skills you will need two to three years out NOW. Start acquiring skills that will be the building blocks for the roles that do not exist today and will emerge deeper in the decade, NOW.

Back to the concept of sustainable receipts. One of the biggest challenges you will face in being hyper-relevant is figuring out not only what skills you need, but more importantly, why, when, and how to get them. As a lecturer with top-tier and elite universities and a graduate of a prestigious top-tier institution of higher learning, what I am about to tell you may be shocking, but it's the truth. The future of work is all about skills. It is about how you build them, stack them, augment them, leverage them, where you get them and whether they are portable. Having said that, simply building your strategy around an undergraduate or graduate degree will not be enough. A college degree reigns and will for some time be a minimum requirement for most jobs. I get that. However, you need what I call skill and credential plugins to stay relevant and amplify your brand.

I will use my journey as an example. I have a doctorate in education with a focus on organizational change and leadership. My research centered on the future of work. Although I have two other graduate degrees in business and marketing, I needed plugins to solidify my expertise in the future of work. So, I completed micro-credentials in AI business strategy from MIT and in data analytics from Cornell University. Both are what I call micro-credential plugins. The work I do with organizations, falls under the domain of human resources. My expertise sits at the intersection of the future of work, AI and the impact on business and people strategies. But, prior to consulting,

I worked in marketing and had no formal background in human resources. So, years ago I added the SHRM-CP, PHR, HCS and SWP human resource industry credential plugins for credibility and completed a certificate in human resources from an Ivy League university. Data science falls into the category of a skill I must have two years from now, so this year, I started taking courses in data science. Issues around AI ethics and algorithmic bias in the workplace are garnering more attention and emerging as critical issues for organizations. So, I completed courses to increase my knowledge and competency in both areas. Solid skills in data science, AI ethics and algorithmic bias will serve as building blocks for the skills that I will need three to four years from now for roles that do not exist today. There are also other things I need to know and understand that have interesting intersectionality with my work and that add context and further competitively position my brand. Two examples are the neuroscience of leadership and the humanization of work. So, I also completed LinkedIn Learning courses in neuroscience and became a Workhuman® Certified Professional. For context, these are my receipts. The figure below will help you visualize the role and continuum of now, next, and future skills.

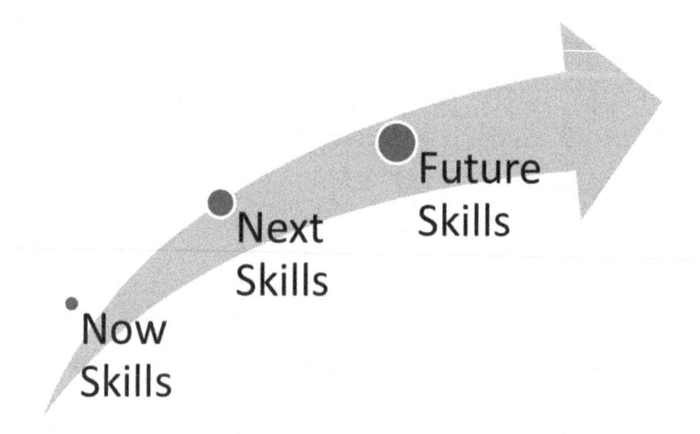

Figure 2. Now, Next, and Future Skills

You will need to approach the process of being hyper-relevant with relative precision to acquire now, next, and future skills and competencies. You can do it! Pause for a moment and think about these questions:

1. What do I need to learn to amplify and future-proof my brand?
2. When and at what intervals do I need to acquire the skills I need to stay ahead of the future?
3. Where will I acquire the specific skills, certifications, and credentials I need that align with my brand and position me to thrive on my terms?
4. Why do I need to acquire new skills to amplify my brand? What's my end game?
5. How will I apply, integrate, or combine new functional, hybrid, hard, soft, technical, and software skills to competitively position my brand for the future?

HOW YOU GET THERE

To begin the process of developing your plan for hyper-relevancy in the future of work and acquiring sustainable receipts, start here:

- **Think**, act, and perform like a futurist
- **Learn** strategic foresight and identify future scenarios in which you can thrive
- **Use** relevant emerging industry, job cluster and skills data
- **Reckon** with the fact that all of us have skills gaps – own yours

- **Understand** the what, when, why and how of what you need to learn
- **Identify** the skills you need using my now, next, future model
- **Leverage** data, predictive analytics, and AI platforms to your advantage
- **Map out learning**: employer-sponsored, degrees, micro-credentials, certificates, industry credentials, LinkedIn Learning, Coursera, immersive learning, bootcamps, thought leaders
- **Develop** your skill up timeline and collect reputable, portable, sustainable receipts

Be less afraid of what it takes for you to be hyper-relevant than you are of being insignificant in the future of work.

Dr. Terri Horton
FUTURIST

PERSONAL REFLECTION

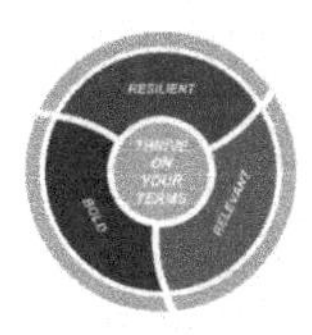

The purpose of this reflection is to explore what hyper-relevancy will mean for you and what you are willing to do to achieve it.

1. What excites you or frightens you about learning to think, act and perform like a futurist so that the future of work is not your force majeure?
2. Using the now, next, future skills model, how would you describe your level of relevancy or hyper-relevancy?
3. What challenges might you face in prioritizing your skill up plan? How will you mitigate them?
4. How long do you believe it will take to acquire the skills you need in each category? What skills from each category will you specifically need?
5. What resources will you need to develop, finance, and complete your skill up plan?

YOUR THRIVE PLAN

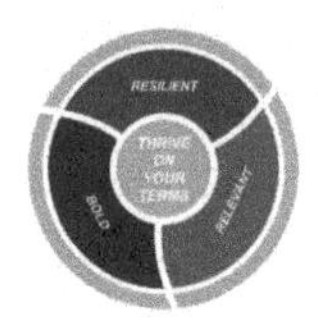

Part 3 "Hyper-Relevancy and Sustainable Receipts"

For the third part of your plan, you will identify three goals and actions related to skilling up and becoming hyper-relevant. Identify three goals, key actions, desired results, resources, skills, knowledge or training, networking or partnerships required, an accountability partner, and a relevant timeline. Most importantly, identify how each goal and related actions get you closer to owning the future of work on your terms!

THRIVE PLAN

GOAL

GOAL & TIMELINE

RESOURCES

ACCOUNTABILITY PARTNER

DESIRED OUTCOMES & SUCCESS MEASUREMENTS

HOW GOAL SUPPORTS THRIVING

THRIVE PLAN

GOAL

GOAL & TIMELINE

RESOURCES

ACCOUNTABILITY PARTNER

DESIRED OUTCOMES & SUCCESS MEASUREMENTS

HOW GOAL SUPPORTS THRIVING

THRIVE PLAN

GOAL

GOAL & TIMELINE

RESOURCES

ACCOUNTABILITY PARTNER

DESIRED OUTCOMES & SUCCESS MEASUREMENTS

HOW GOAL SUPPORTS THRIVING

THRIVE PLAN NOTES

PART 3
"HYPER-RELEVANCY AND SUSTAINABLE RECEIPTS"

5
BE AUDACIOUSLY BOLD

Unapologetically Pursue New and Reimagined Possibilities

"The present moment contains past and future.
The secret of transformation is in the way
we handle this very moment."

—Thich Nhat Hanh—

Southeast Asia and Magnus

I arrived at the airport after eighteen hours of flying just before midnight in March of 2015. It was hot and humid, even at that hour. I was trading on adrenaline, exhaustion, excitement, and trepidation. I looked through a sea of people for my driver holding the sign with my name. I found him and followed him. We didn't talk much, not just because it was late, but because we didn't speak the same language. As the driver sped through the streets to the hotel, I was drawn in by the captivating vitality of the city. I remember saying to myself, "Wow, you really did this!" When I arrived at the hotel where I would stay for two weeks, I reflected on how I got there. A month before, late on a Saturday night, I received an email from the director of an executive MBA program in Vietnam. In the email, he explained that the professor scheduled to teach the accelerated course had fallen ill and could not return to Vietnam. He explained that the university would pay for all travel expenses, including a 5-star hotel, meals, incidentals, and a five-figure salary for teaching the course. To allay fears about authenticity, he explained how he found me and included links to the university's website and international program along with his contact information and links to his social media profiles.

Initially, I was extremely skeptical. I thought the email was spam, and just as I was going to press the delete button, I paused and thought, if this is not spam, what a badass opportunity! After further investigation, it was clear that it indeed was a real opportunity. So, I took a leap of faith, and boldly departed for Vietnam, alone no less, to begin the adventure.

While I had traveled extensively throughout the world, I had never been to Ho Chi Minh City or Hanoi, Vietnam. It turned out to be one of the most remarkable experiences of my life and set the stage for future opportunities with international audiences. Within twelve months, I was invited to return and teach the course in Vietnam two more times. Vietnam left an indelible mark on my soul and is one of my favorite places on the planet. I would not have experienced the beauty of the country and people or developed relationships that continued long after I returned had I not been audaciously and unapologetically bold.

The year before, I was one of two women taking a class about 50 miles east of Los Angeles. There were fifteen students in the class taught by two rather intimidating ex-marines. The first day of training went great. The second day, not so much. You see, I was having a difficult time wrapping my head around the coordination of coming to a smooth and complete stop. I just couldn't do it. When prompted to stop, I would freeze up, skid, and go beyond the stopping point. Let me say, learning to stop without skidding was absolutely critical. After the second day of training, on the drive home, wondering if I would pass the course, I remember asking myself, Are you crazy? Are you really going to do this? Why don't you just quit?

Just as tears were about to drop from my weary eyes, I paused, turned up the radio, put on my sunglasses, and smiled. The answer was a resounding Hell Yeah! I later passed the class, got my Class M driver's license, and bought my Harley Davidson. It was a Road Glide, a big bike, and it was purple, one of my favorite colors. I named it Magnus, meaning "Great" in Latin. I loved that bike for so many reasons, not just because of how free and limitless it felt to ride. Most importantly, I loved it because it was a reminder of how I decided to be unapologetically bold enough to check it off my bucket list. Although I sold it a few years later, it fueled a deeper meaning of how I conceptualized audacity and boldness. It too, left an indelible mark on my soul.

While I've acted boldly throughout most of my personal and professional life, my experiences in Vietnam and with Magnus taught me the meaning of real unapologetic, audacious boldness. The experiences taught me that real audacity and boldness could push me in new ways to move past the trepidation of the unknown and thrust me into the unimaginable, all of which could serve as a catalyst for discovering a multitude of new possibilities. Harnessing the dynamism of audacious boldness drove me to apply to speak at a global summit at Oxford University, deliver a TEDx talk, take courses in data science, start a new line of business during the pandemic and even write this book. As this decade continues to roll out, audacious boldness will continue to drive me towards new profoundly empowering and innovative opportunities to engage with people, organizations, and learning institutions across the globe. Whether I do this in person, as a hologram, or as an avatar in the metaverse, I will do it and thrive on my own terms.

We lived through unimaginable events in 2020, but we made it through! Think about how resilient we are! Think about how boldly we pressed through uncertainty! I cannot tell you what being audaciously bold will look like for you. It may be a series of behaviors and actions that push you beyond the scope of what you envision for yourself or seizing a catalyzing spectacular opportunity. What I do know is that it must push you beyond your limits of comfort, seem unimaginable, scare you and subsequently make you say, Hell Yeah, I am going to do this! You must be bold NOW! I want you to be bold enough to eradicate the possibility of a force majeure in your life! The question is, how audaciously bold will you be in not only reimagining possibilities but, more importantly, making them come to life on your terms?

The Business of Boldness is Human

The business of boldness is driven by explosive growth, AI-driven innovation, an audacious focus on people, and humanizing work as organizations battle to win the race for what is next between now and 2030. The business of boldness, in my view, is centered in part on amplifying the position of the Business Roundtable's reimagined purpose of a corporation. The Business Roundtable represents the CEOs of leading corporations in the United States. In 2019, Jaime Diamond, Chairman of the Business Roundtable, released a bold new statement on the purpose of a corporation. The bold new purpose was a clear shift from operating for the sole purpose of serving shareholders to committing to leading organizations for the benefit of customers, employees, suppliers, communities, and shareholders. Did you notice the order of priority? In the announcement Chairman, Jaime Diamond explained the rationale for the shift:

"The American dream is alive, but fraying. Major employers are investing in their workers and communities because they know it is the only way to be successful over the long term. These modernized principles reflect the business community's unwavering commitment to continue to push for an economy that serves all."

Need more proof that the business of boldness is human? The 2021 Deloitte Human Capital Trends report reinforced that organizations that win and dominate in the future epitomize a thrive mindset and create new realities on their terms. Sound familiar? Let's take a peek into the report:

"In today's world of perpetual disruption, it's time for organizations to shift from a *survive* mindset to a *thrive* mindset. Making this shift depends on an organization's becoming—and remaining—distinctly human at its core, because today's environment of extreme dynamism calls for a degree of courage, judgment, and flexibility that only humans can bring." It is a different way of being that approaches every question, every issue, and every decision from a human angle first."

Both the Business Roundtable and the Deloitte Report describe the urgency of audaciously bold shifts! The audaciously bold shift in prioritizing people to drive growth and innovation this decade will far eclipse today's data-driven people strategies centered on productivity, performance, engagement, and development. The new archetype of people strategies will mimic consumer brand experiences. They will extend more profoundly into the values, interests, needs, social, equity, wellness, and environmental priorities of employees, customers, and communities. This is how audaciously bold companies will attract and retain the best talent and grow into the future. To a large extent, this archetype's connective tissue began to fuse with bone, so to speak, in 2020 as organizations were forced to examine and address long-overlooked issues of social justice, equity, income inequality, the environment, work-life harmony, and well-being with unprecedented accountability.

As we move through the decade, bold everything will drive the redesign of organizations. Everything from bold growth to bold futuristic tech, to bold innovation and bold experiences for workers, customers, and stakeholders, will be normalized and embedded in transformation strategies of audaciously bold future-focused organizations. Prioritizing people means that jobs will be designed for purpose, lifestyle, mobility, and impact. Prioritizing people means that organizations will continue to boldly shift, as described in the Harvard Business Review from dated corporate social responsibility models to a new framework of corporate justice responsibility. This shift aligns with the Business Roundtable's restated purpose of a corporation and drives positive social and equitable change inside and outside of organizations.

Workhuman®, a platform dedicated to helping organizations prioritize the human experience in the workplace, created a framework, that in my view, exemplifies the bold expectations of the Millennial, Gen Z, and Alpha employees who will dominate the workforce by 2030. This model also connects the experiential dots that extend strategies across people, customers, and communities. The model prioritizes:

- Meaningful Work
- Gratitude and Recognition
- Growth
- Inclusion and Belonging
- Work-Life Harmony
- Fair Pay
- Sustainability
- Privacy
- Safety

The business of boldness in the future of work is unapologetically, audaciously, and boldly human. The imperative to prioritize people, customers, and communities as a core business strategy will transcend geography, industry, role, and status. Some of the most provocative shifts hailed from compelling global research on the future of work prove that a bold approach to humanizing work indeed will prevail. Imagine working and experiencing health-screening lounges, self-contained air purifying plant walls that promote well-being, occupancy visualization, heat mapping and holographic global team meetings. Imagine AI Alexa-style managers, coaches, and assistants. Imagine, if you will, AI that drives an inclusive, mindful, and emotionally intelligent work culture that inspires human potential and empowers human capital to thrive! I want you to be audaciously bold enough to pivot, shift, and adapt so that you are prepared to thrive as the business of boldness becomes more human!

WHAT YOU NEED TO DO

The first thing you need to do is get your head in the game and realize that boldness can position you to thwart a force majeure! My father was a paratrooper in the 82nd Airborne, and he taught me that sometimes you just need to jump! I want you to jump into boldness! This decade demands audacity and boldness, period. Why does it demand audacity and boldness? It demands them because you will need the acuity to rethink and reimagine what a career, work, job, and even purpose means to you in the framework of what you want for your life.

You will need to be bold enough to stare change in the face and not fold. You will need to be bold enough to dare. Yes, dare to embrace the part of the "This is Your Life" Holstee Manifesto that says, "This is your life! Live your dream and share your passion."

You will need to audaciously believe that your boldness will be the catalyst for experiencing unimaginable possibilities...even if those possibilities are not in your line of sight today. You will need to be bold enough to do the heavy lifting of continuous skilling up, leveling up, and reinventing.

You will need to be audacious enough to determine what working and living on your terms means and not let fear or the voices of those who are not yet bold enough to do the same deter you. You will need the audacity to think boldly, the boldness to act, perform, and create in new ways, and to unapologetically commit to winning and thriving by your design and on your terms!

Figure 3. Audacious, Bold, Unapologetic, New Possibilities

HOW YOU GET THERE

To begin the process of developing your plan to become more audaciously and unapologetically bold start here:

- **Stop** seeing yourself through a myopic lens and focus on what you can become
- **Stop** feeling safe and content in what is familiar and comfortable – Change your mindset to avert a force majeure
- **Determine** what audacity and boldness can mean to you – What are your terms?
- **Imagine** how you will bridge your talent and passions with emerging panoramas
- **Embrace** fluidity, free agency, and entrepreneurship as strategies for boldness
- **Create** an ecosystem that supports and empowers audacity and boldness

When I was a child, my grandmother told me I could become anything I wanted to be. So I took her up on it by living boldly!

Dr. Terri Horton
FUTURIST

PERSONAL REFLECTION

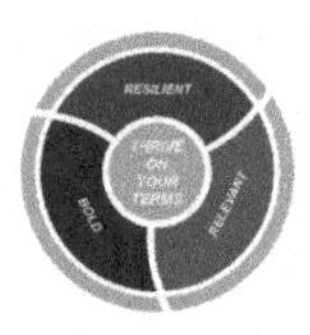

The purpose of this reflection is to uncover your strengths and opportunities for development so that you can leverage audacity and boldness to thrive on your terms.

1. How do you define audacity and boldness?
2. When you think about being audaciously bold, what new possibilities come to mind?
3. How might audacity and boldness align with your sense of purpose?
4. As you transform your thinking and mindset, what might impede your ability to be audaciously bold? How will you mitigate impediments?
5. What actions will you take to be audaciously and unapologetically bold?

YOUR THRIVE PLAN

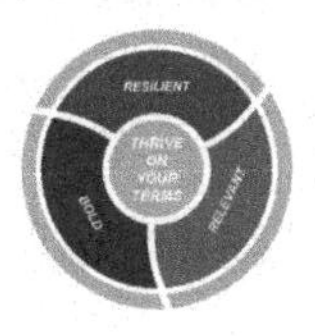

Part 4 "Audaciously and Unapologetically Pursue New and Reimagined Possibilities"

For the fourth part of your plan, you will identify three goals and actions related to becoming audaciously and unapologetically bold. Identify three goals, key actions, desired results, resources, skills, knowledge or training, networking or partnerships required, an accountability partner, and a relevant timeline. Most importantly, identify how each goal and related actions get you closer to owning the future of work on your terms!

THRIVE PLAN

GOAL

GOAL & TIMELINE

RESOURCES

ACCOUNTABILITY PARTNER

DESIRED OUTCOMES & SUCCESS MEASUREMENTS

HOW GOAL SUPPORTS THRIVING

THRIVE PLAN

GOAL

GOAL & TIMELINE

RESOURCES

ACCOUNTABILITY PARTNER

DESIRED OUTCOMES & SUCCESS MEASUREMENTS

HOW GOAL SUPPORTS THRIVING

THRIVE PLAN

GOAL

GOAL & TIMELINE

RESOURCES

ACCOUNTABILITY PARTNER

DESIRED OUTCOMES & SUCCESS MEASUREMENTS

HOW GOAL SUPPORTS THRIVING

THRIVE PLAN NOTES

PART 4
"AUDACIOUSLY AND UNAPOLOGETICALLY PURSUE NEW AND REIMAGINED POSSIBILITIES"

6
THRIVE ON YOUR TERMS

Thriving on Your Terms is Your Power and Your Future

"The question is not how to survive,
but how to thrive with passion, compassion, and style."

—Maya Angelou—

Purpose and Intention

Please repeat after me aloud...Thriving on my own terms is my power and my future! Words have power and what we say to ourselves and believe is powerful. That is why I wanted you to say those words aloud audaciously! To thrive and own your future, you must be intentional. To thrive is to be intentional. To thrive, your intention must be immersed in purpose. Purpose and intention will enable you to keep moving forward. Intention will fuel you to take action when you feel frozen. Purpose will force you to make the tough decisions and make the sacrifices you need to thrive as the future of work continues to dynamically reveal itself. On your terms means that you harness the power of agency to catalyze your purpose and intentions. Agency will also enable you to shift, pivot, and unapologetically reinvent YOU.

Not sure if you know how to thrive? Think about where we've been, what we've experienced, what we've witnessed and all that we unlearned, reconciled, reanimated, and created, just to survive in 2020. The COVID-19 pandemic and the pressures of 2020 wreaked havoc in some way across the lives of most, delivered in the form of disruption to work, health, finances, or relationships. Yet, according to the American Psychological Association, 71% of Americans remained hopeful about the future! Yes, we did that! Those of us who made it through 2020 mastered surviving with an eye for thriving beyond the chaos, beyond the pain, beyond the stressors. We did it with purpose and intention!

Think of this: you mastered surviving even if where you are, what you do, or how you live is vastly different and even if your circle of friends and loved ones is smaller than before 2020. In many regards, we learned how to thrive in our own little contexts despite overwhelming limitations and boundaries and for many, even through excruciating pain, and loss. We learned how to etch out little ways to thrive, both large and small, without realizing it. That's right, and we just thought we were figuring out ways to survive. Within twelve months of first learning of the pandemic, we lived through rapid and radical change, shock, fear, uncertainty, unprecedented political and social unrest and unimaginable events and circumstances.

Let's pause on this for a moment. Nearly every aspect of our lives was upended by the events and circumstances of 2020. We lived through a pandemic that claimed millions of lives across the globe, shifted to working remotely, homeschooling, virtual and drive-by birthdays, graduations, and holidays. We lived through social distancing and isolation, a global recession, Brexit, and devastating wildfires in Australia and California. We lived through a global social justice movement, the postponement of the 2020 Summer Olympics and Coachella, and the death of fashion! We experienced the election of the first female African American and South Asian vice-president of the United States and the United States Capitol storming. We witnessed an investment phenomenon driven by millennials and Gen Z that nearly became a force majeure of sorts for traditional hedge fund companies and a popular trading platform. We experienced and witnessed the crisis of women from the executive suite to the mailroom exiting the workplace in unprecedented numbers due to the multiple competing priorities of working from home, balancing careers, and homeschooling. And, just as the COVID-19 vaccine was being delivered into the arms of people across the world, new COVID-19 variants emerged. Yet, in our quest to ascribe meaning to our new reality, find a new way forward and protect and nurture our mental health we skilled up. We became creators and innovators. We indulged in more self-care, found new ways to connect with loved ones, adopted more animals, got hooked on plants, became bike riders, skaters, meditators, and affirmers of self-worth. We cooked, we exercised more and creatively redesigned our homes into multi-purpose living spaces. We traveled virtually through museums, zoos, countries, and even through space. Yes, we did all these things to find some way to thrive despite our circumstances. In many cases, we did all of this while working, managing families, caring for loved ones, and taking on additional responsibilities while uncertain about our future and when, how, and if we would return to pre-pandemic normality. So, do not speak the words or allow yourself to believe that you cannot find ways to thrive on your terms and mean it and live it.

I surprised myself and started a couple of hobbies during this time as well. I didn't plan to start them. I would never have been able to convince myself prior that I had time to indulge in them. However, to my surprise, they just emerged organically, almost like a coping mechanism, I suppose. I began hydroponic gardening, coloring, and fusion cooking. Let me say that nothing in my past suggested that I would ever start or fall in love with doing any of these things. In fact, I suck at growing things so much that all the plants in my home were artificial until we were well into the pandemic. I had not colored in coloring books since I was a child, and my view on cooking was purely utilitarian, as I preferred food prep, meal delivery, and restaurants. Although my newfound interests were surprising, to say the least, they added elements of excitement and dimension to my life during that tumultuous time. I approached them with purpose and intention.

Like most others, I was on a personal quest to cope with our new reality and thrive despite pandemic-driven limitations and boundaries. I made myself find a way to do all of these things while concurrently managing my consulting business, lecturing, taking courses, and writing this book. The first bonus I received from all of this was delightful. My partner, family, and friends were super supportive and excited about the hydroponic gardening and fusion cooking. Their excitement and support served as an accelerant for thriving with these new hobbies to the point that I no longer refer to them as hobbies. They are embedded and part of my overarching purpose and intentionality for how I live. The second bonus was that I realized that hydroponic gardening, cooking, and coloring were extensions of my authentic self and were demonstrative of the same purpose that drives my work. That purpose is grounded in nurturing, developing, empowering people and things, and creating and reimagining possibilities. It was an example of harmonizing my purpose, passion, and interests in new areas of my life. The third bonus was fire! You see, I am really good at analogous thinking. So, in between my work, writing, gardening, and cooking, a new business idea materialized. It emerged one day when I accidentally placed an orchid too close to the hydroponic machine. It's a long story, so I'll get right to the point. In a nutshell, it's a new line of business that will provide a platform for vibrant aging workers to thrive as they face both the complexities and exciting possibilities of this decade. I found a path on my terms to etch out little ways to thrive during the pandemic while managing the uncertainty and complexities of 2020 and the competing priorities of my work and personal life. In the process, I discovered a new business idea for the path forward. The story I shared of my little experience of finding a way to thrive through the pandemic by hydroponic gardening, coloring, and cooking while balancing work, personal priorities, skilling up, writing a book, and discovering a new business model, is just a small example of how the framework of being resilient, relevant, bold, and thriving in the path forward comes together.

I have to work with purpose and intention: it's in my DNA. My life's purpose is to educate, uplift, and empower – it is directly woven into my authentic self. If I were unable to intentionally pursue my purpose through my life's work of educating, uplifting, and empowering directly or tangentially, I would feel disconnected from my authentic self and out of harmony and balance. So being resiliently, relevantly, and boldly connected to my purpose and intention along with balancing relationships, spirituality, and well-being, enables me to thrive on my terms! I want you to thrive on your terms by being resilient, relevant, and bold! I want you to uncover and live what thriving means to you personally and professionally because thriving on your terms indeed will be your power and your future.

Surviving is Out. Thriving Is the New Obsession!

Chapter two of this book laid the groundwork for thinking about the new next and the path forward. If you remember, I wrote about how within the first three to four months of the pandemic, top global consulting firms provided insights on how organizations should shift from focusing on reacting, responding, and surviving the impact to capitalizing on what was learned and focusing on pivoting forward and thriving. Thriving, that is, with purpose and intention for social impact. As organizations continue to pivot out of survival mode, a focus on thriving will be preeminent. Organizations will focus on thriving internally as well as externally. Stakeholder capitalism will be the scaffolding that supports this shift. The new obsession with thriving contextualizes thriving with a positive impact not only on the bottom line but also on workers, customers, partners, communities, and the environment. This obsession is forward-looking and future-facing, and frankly, is an act of long-term strategic sustainability and a competitive force of nature. Yes, purpose and intention squarely aimed at prioritizing social impact will drive the designing and reimagining of organizations, strategy, leadership, worker and customer experiences, partnerships, and collaborations and will define what it means to thrive between now and 2030.

Purpose will drive the shift, and intention will underpin accountability. Just as the events of 2020 were the catalyst for shifts in multiple areas of our lives, they too accelerated the shift to prioritizing organizational impact so that everyone thrives. Thriving by prioritizing positive social impact will drive positive change for equity, create new possibilities for underserved communities, expand supply chains, create unimaginably dynamic global and industry partnerships and collaborations, empower workers, support emotionally intelligent organizational cultures, and humanize the worker experience. We will watch and experience waves of change as this shift vigorously materializes and expands through 2030. Organizations focused on surviving and building intention and purpose around pre-pandemic business nostalgia will struggle to survive in the long term as irrelevant approaches, and business models metastasize through every vein and organ of the enterprise.

In the workplace, thriving for employees will mean more flexibility, choice, shared purpose, and meaningful work. Big data, predictive analytics, and AI will facilitate flexibility, purpose, intention, and consequential work. The traditional nine to five workdays will be a relic. Bots, algorithms, robots, avatars, holograms, virtual and augmented reality, and immersive 3D glasses will be the norm. The work we do will cease to be executed solely on hardware and devices but will be performed using gesture recognition technology activated by voice, hands, and head tracking. Where, what type of work, and how we will work between now and 2030 is being designed today by brilliant futurists, business strategists, data scientists, technologists, architects, urban planners, philosophers, sociologists, economists, and designers. Think of the intelligent environments, experiences, and purposeful work that can emerge from such dynamic and high-powered collaborations aimed at enabling business, people, and societies to thrive.

In full transparency, let me be clear. Not everyone will thrive as the future of work unfolds through this decade. The unfolding will indeed present challenges for both organizations and people, particularly those that have not done the work to avoid a force majeure by being resilient, relevant, and bold. Organizations, people, and entrepreneurs that fail to build resiliency and agility, remain relevant, take bold risks, make bold decisions, and bold moves to shift and pivot into the new next, risk being left behind with an opaque path forward.

There will be industries, businesses, countries, regions and cities that continue to contract, never fully recover from the impact of COVID-19 and fail to shift and pivot to thrive in the COVID-altered future. Statistics suggest that AI and automation will negatively impact women in the workplace. New jobs will be created to replace some of the eliminated positions but will require skills that many may not have. Colleges and universities will continue to experience enrollment declines as they struggle to align programs, curriculum, and student experiences with future of work skill demands and emerging technologies. Digital, educational, and economic divides will continue to be substantial hurdles to overcome for underrepresented and communities of color to thrive through 2030. There will also be portions of the working population who will be permanently underemployed and unemployed because they lack the required skills and experiences. Frankly, there may not be enough room in the future of work landscape for everyone.

As you watch the unfolding of the future of work, this decade can feel both exciting and frightening at the same time. That's ok it should, so that you get your mind in the right place and do the work to avoid a force majeure. My goal is to help you make sure that you are on the right side of the transformation of work so that you can thrive purposefully, intentionally, and on your terms. While no one can predict a full snapshot or panorama of the future of work between now and 2030 with absolute precision, as a workforce futurist, I predict that organizations that are obsessed with being resilient, relevant, and bold, human-centric, and purposefully and intentionally prioritize stakeholder impact will be indisputably positioned to thrive well beyond 2030. Thriving will indeed be the obsession!

WHAT YOU NEED TO DO

Start by defining what thriving on your own terms means to you now and what it will mean to you as you evolve through this decade. The concept of thriving is magnificent, delicious, and rings of defiance. In fact, the thought of thriving on your own terms is downright sexy! But before we unpack this process, let's take a meditative pause so that you can absorb what it will take to contemplate and prepare for the expedition into thriving on your own terms through 2030. Review the questions purposefully and intentionally. Give yourself permission to be vulnerable. Answer authentically.

- Are you prepared to define what thriving on your own terms means in new contexts, new environments, and, in the unrecognizable, despite the background noise streaming from your head, the cacophony of extraneous voices of doubt seeping into your ears from family, friends, and colleagues?
- Are you prepared to make bold decisions and take bold actions that others will question and may not understand until years later as you reimagine your future?
- Are you prepared to reset, stretch, reinvent, and emerge as your most audaciously, purposeful, intentional, and unapologetic self to experience unimaginable possibilities?
- Are you prepared to recognize yourself as someone completely different from who you are and who you thought you should be? Would you recognize yourself in the future as an algorithmic bias officer, AI psychologist, quantum data analyst, space tour guide, or even a climate change response leader?

Trust me, I know it is a lot! But, if you answered the questions in the affirmative, then you are prepared to begin building the casting you will need to shape and sculpt the YOU who will grandly show up. The YOU who will be malleable enough to reset, stretch, reinvent, and re-emerge time after time on your terms. The shaped and sculpted YOU who is authentic, extremely confident and knows that thriving on your terms is your power. Yes, the resilient, relevant, and bold YOU who will thrive purposefully and intentionally in the future of work.

Thriving on your terms through 2030 requires that you harmonize your expertise, judgment, insight, matchlessness, and superpowers to create your own opportunities. This iterative process of shaping and molding will be challenging and will have peaks and valleys, ebbs, and flows. But you must keep moving forward in defining and preparing your path as you move through the future. You will need coping mechanisms.

There will be times when you think you cannot take another step, or you just cannot learn another new ANYTHING! There will be times when you are gripped by the fear of uncertainty and doubt that you have the capacity for boldness. However, that's when your unabashed drive to avoid a force majeure will kick in. That's when you will cash in on your currencies of emotional intelligence and resilience. In fact, that's when the pure irresistibility of being hyper-relevant and thinking like a futurist will propel you. That's when your unadulterated desire to explore and experience new and reimagined possibilities will surface and kick into overdrive. And yes, that is when you will remember and rationalize that thriving on your own terms is your power and future. Humanize the process for yourself as you define and design how you will thrive. Be good to yourself, position spirituality, well-being, relationships, and self-care as priorities throughout the journey. Let this decade be your obsession! After all, if not now…then when?

HOW YOU GET THERE

To begin the process of developing your plan to thrive on your own terms, start here:

- **Identify** your true authentic purpose and how it can be harmonized personally and professionally
- **Define** your intentions and create the mapping for pursuing your purpose
- **Imagine** what thriving on your own terms will mean to you between now and 2025 and between 2025 and 2030

- **Commit** to resilience, relevancy, and boldness in your pursuit of thriving
- **Bolster** thriving with well-being, spirituality, learning, relationships, and impact
- **Integrate** your thrive plans and execute

Want to thrive on your terms?

Purposefully put your authentic self to work...then pay yourself well!

Dr. Terri Horton
FUTURIST

PERSONAL REFLECTION

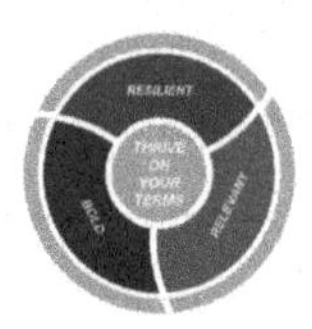

The purpose of this reflection is to explore what thriving on your terms will mean for you, identify considerations and pinpoint what you are willing to do to purposely and intentionally thrive.

1. Describe your authentic self. What is your purpose? How might you serve that purpose with impact in the future?
2. Which intentions will you leverage to catalyze your purpose?
3. Describe how harmonizing your authentic self with purpose, intention, and impact materializes for you on your terms between now and 2030.
4. How will thriving on your own terms propel you through 2030? What does thriving on your terms mean to you?
5. What role will your goals play in being resilient, relevant, bold and your ability to thrive on your terms in the future?

YOUR THRIVE PLAN

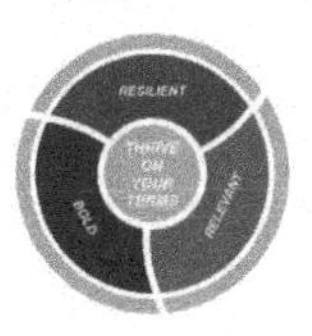

Part 5 "Thriving on Your Terms is Your Power and Your Future"

For the fifth part of your plan, you will identify three goals and actions related to thriving on your terms, in your power, for your future. Identify three goals, key actions, desired results, resources, skills, knowledge or training, networking or partnerships required, an accountability partner, and a relevant timeline. Most importantly, identify how each goal and related actions get you closer to owning the future of work on your terms!

THRIVE PLAN

GOAL

GOAL & TIMELINE

RESOURCES

ACCOUNTABILITY PARTNER

DESIRED OUTCOMES & SUCCESS MEASUREMENTS

HOW GOAL SUPPORTS THRIVING

THRIVE PLAN

GOAL

GOAL & TIMELINE

RESOURCES

ACCOUNTABILITY PARTNER

DESIRED OUTCOMES & SUCCESS MEASUREMENTS

HOW GOAL SUPPORTS THRIVING

THRIVE PLAN

GOAL

GOAL & TIMELINE

RESOURCES

ACCOUNTABILITY PARTNER

DESIRED OUTCOMES & SUCCESS MEASUREMENTS

HOW GOAL SUPPORTS THRIVING

THRIVE PLAN NOTES

PART 5
"THRIVING ON YOUR TERMS IS YOUR POWER AND YOUR FUTURE"

7

YOUR THRIVE PLAN

No Force Majeure Clause in the Future of Work – Live Your Plan

"Success is only meaningful and enjoyable if it feels like your own."

—Michelle Obama—

In this book, I use the term force majeure as a metaphor. In the introduction, I described one of my experiences with a large client contract that included a force majeure clause. I shared the angst that I felt at the thought of a disruptive, unforeseen circumstance or act of God triggering the force majeure clause, therefore rendering the contract void, preventing me from working with the client and receiving a five-figure consulting fee. Using the phrase as a metaphor, I explained why the future of work would be a force majeure for most. It should be no surprise then that I will end this book with an extension of the conversation about the future of work and how its manifestation could trigger a force majeure by canceling your ability to thrive on your terms. So, let's level set here. There are no force majeure clauses in the future of work to protect or insulate you from being impacted or canceled.

For emphasis and staging, I will help you rationalize this on a deeper level. I'll first unpack this with a brief discussion about real force majeure clauses and why they do not apply to all disruptive, unforeseen, and uncontrollable triggering events, not even a pandemic. I'll metaphorically reinforce why a force majeure clause will not protect you from the radical workforce transformation you will experience through 2030. I'll wrap up with why your ability to be resilient, relevant, and bold will position you to solidify your future, discover new possibilities, and thrive on your terms.

The American Bar Association describes a force majeure as an event, circumstance, or occurrence that can trigger a contract's cancelation. The force majeure clause protects both parties if the triggering event warrants canceling the contract, thereby protecting both parties. Now let's apply the concept of the force majeure clause to the COVID-19 pandemic. One would logically assume that the pandemic indeed was a force majeure. Right? Well, think again, as the answer is opaque. The American Bar Association provided clarity on force majeure clauses and the applicability to the pandemic. Surprisingly, the rationale was that whether the pandemic could be recognized as an event to trigger the force majeure clause depended on how the clause was written and the language used in the contract.

Let me break this down for you. Think of concerts, flights and hotel reservations that were canceled due to the pandemic. During the first few months of the pandemic, tens of thousands of travelers were forced to cancel flights and hotel reservations. I was one of them. I was scheduled to speak at a global conference held at Oxford University in April and faced the same dilemma when travel from the United States to the United Kingdom was banned. The pandemic, in many cases, did not meet the measure of force majeure clauses. I was fortunate to recover some of my costs. I was one of the lucky ones. While the force majeure clauses from the airline and hotel partially protected me, they did not make me whole. Let's look at another example. I remember hearing about candidates deep in the job selection process, with one or two steps remaining, informed that the selection process was abruptly paused, absent the hope of rescheduling. The pandemic was the triggering event that caused the force majeure in these examples. Got it?

Let's focus again on the future of work and the force majeure metaphor. If you think that you can magically activate a force majeure clause as you roll through the future of work when you face disruption, displacement, or are forced to reinvent, you will be devastatingly disappointed. Let me be clear, no one will go unscathed. In 2017, Dr. Andrew Ng, Stanford University professor, scientist, architect of Google's AI strategy and co-founder of Coursera said, "Just as electricity transformed almost everything 100 years ago, today I actually have a hard time thinking of an industry that I don't think AI will transform in the next several years." That was before the COVID-19 pandemic, and we know that the pandemic and events of 2020 accelerated everything! So technically, most people are already behind as they blindly await their impending force majeure. You must shift and pivot. You must do the work to prepare for the future you want and deserve.

Let's go deeper. Rewind and go back in time to 2020. If you remember, during the pandemic, even in most cases, federal and state interventions did not mitigate staggering unemployment, business closures, bankruptcies, foreclosures, or evictions. Despite billions of dollars used to prop up Americans and insulate them from the financial impacts of the pandemic, sadly, many were still left behind. Comparatively, as we move through this decade turbo-charged by AI and automation and work is reimagined, there will not be enough interventions from employers, government agencies, foundations, nonprofits, or other safety nets to make millions of displaced, underemployed, or unemployed workers whole. If the worse pandemic to hit the globe in 100 years was not enough to trigger and activate real force majeure clauses to legally protect millions of businesses, displaced workers, and entrepreneurs around the world from financial losses, business closures, bankruptcy, and unemployment, do not foolishly believe that there will be a figurative force majeure clause of sorts in the future of work to protect you and make you whole if you are ill-prepared.

I titled this book Force Majeure because I wanted you to understand that what you experience on your journey through the future of work does not have to be an unforeseeable, uncontrollable or a potentially catastrophic series of events. I want you to get excited about the future of work, because you are going to custom design it for yourself on your terms. You now have the tools you need to begin the design process. You have the power to do that! You have the power to do more than survive the future of work. You have the power to thrive – know it and believe it!

This book's purpose was for you to learn that there are steps and actions you must take with precision to make sure that the future of work does not become your force majeure. As you moved through the chapters, you read my experiences, strategies, perspectives and received my guidance. You learned how industries and organizations responded to the events of 2020 and how they are responding to and driving ground-breaking change for the future of work. In each chapter, you learned what you need to do and the actions you need to take to begin the journey to be resilient, relevant, bold and thrive. You reflected on critical questions that prepared you to develop three goals for each chapter, aimed at cementing your ability to be resilient, relevant, bold, and thrive on your terms. You learned that emotional intelligence and resilience are the currencies more valuable than any cryptocurrency will be in the future. You learned a framework for thinking, acting, and performing like a futurist, being hyper-relevant and collecting sustainable receipts to prove your relevancy. You learned that to be bold, you must audaciously and unapologetically pursue novel and innovative possibilities. Finally, you learned that thriving on your own terms is your power and your future.

I want you to be empowered as you create actionable strategies that enable you to attain the goals you set for yourself in this book. I want you to bet on yourself and hedge your bets by committing to thriving authentically and unapologetically on your terms between now and 2030. The vision and story are yours to create and write. *You are the architect of your future.* You now have the tools to reimagine it, design it, and live it boldly on your terms. The future is waiting for you!

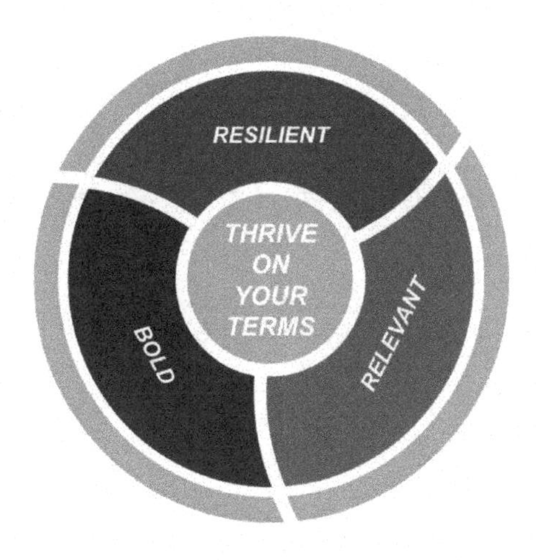

Be resilient, relevant and bold now. Your future self will thank you for the work you began today that enabled you to thrive on your terms!

Dr. Terri Horton
FUTURIST

NOTES

Introduction

1 World Economic Forum, "Resetting the Future of Work Agenda: Disruption and Renewal in a Post-COVID World," White Paper, October 2020, *http://www3.weforum.org/docs/WEF_NES_ Resetting_FOW_Agenda_2020.pdf*

2 Erica Volini and Garth Andrus, "The Future of Work is Here – Here's How Your Organization Needs to Change", Talent Economy, January 18, 2018, *https://www.chieflearningofficer.com/2018/01/18/future-of-work/*

Chapter 1

3 Ernst & Young Global-Strategy and Transformation "The CEO Imperative: Is your strategy set for take-off?" *https://www.ey.com/en_gl/strategy/the-ceo-imperative-is-your-strategy-set-for-take-off*

4 Kevin Sneader and Bob Sternfels, "From surviving to thriving: Reimagining the post-COVID-19 return," McKinsey and Company. May 1, 2020, *https://www.mckinsey.com/featured-insights/future-of-work/from-surviving-to-thriving-reimagining-the-post-covid-19-return*

5 Deloitte Insights, "The Fourth Industrial Revolution: At the intersection of readiness and responsibility, January 2020, *https://www2.deloitte.com/content/dam/Deloitte/de/Documents/human-capital/Deloitte_Review_26_Fourth_Industrial_Revolution.pdf*

6 Annette LaPrade, Janet Mertens, Tanya Moore, and Amy Wright, "The Enterprise Guide to Closing the Skills Gap," IBM, 2019, *https://www.ibm.com/downloads/cas/EPYMNBJA*

7 James McQuivey, Phd, J. P. Gownder and David Johnson, "The Future of Work Starts Now – Four Shocks Will Sort Out the Winners From The Losers in The 2020s", Forrester, April 14, 2020, *https://www.forrester.com/report/The+CEOs+Guide+To+The+Future+Of+Work/-/E-RES160356*

8 J.P. Gownder, "To Build an Adaptive Enterprise, Build An Adaptive Workforce," Forrester, July 25, 2019, *https://go.forrester.com/blogs/the-future-of-work-is-an-adaptive-workforce/*

9 Erica Volini and Garth Andrus, "The Future of Work is Here – Here's How Your Organization Needs to Change", Talent Economy, January 18, 2018, *https://www.chieflearningofficer.com/2018/01/18/future-of-work/*

10 Kim Parker, Rachel Minkin and Jesse Bennett, "Economic Fallout From COVID-19 Continues to Hit Lower-Income Americans Hardest", Pew Research, September 24, 2020, *https://www.pewresearch.org/social-trends/2020/09/24/economic-fallout-from-covid-19-continues-to-hit-lower-income-americans-the-hardest/*

Chapter 2

11 Kevin Sneader and Shubham Singhal,"Beyond the Coronavirus: The path to the next normal" McKinsey and Company, March 23, 2020, *https://www.mckinsey.com/industries/healthcare-systems-and-services/our-insights/beyond-coronavirus-the-path-to-the-next-normal*

12 McKinsey and Company, "COVID-19: Briefing Materials – Global Health and Crisis Response", October 30, 2020, *https://*

www.mckinsey.com/~/media/McKinsey/Business%20Functions/Risk/Our%20Insights/COVID%2019%20Implications%20for%20business/2020%20updates/COVID%2019%20Nov%2011/COVID-19-Facts-and-Insights-Oct-30-Final.pdf

13 McKinsey and Company, "COVID-19 Implications for Business Executive Briefing", March 24, 2021, *https://www.mckinsey.com/business-functions/risk/our-insights/covid-19-implications-for-business*

14 Accenture, "Outmaneuver uncertainty: Navigating the human and business impact of Covid-19", July 31, 2020, *https://www.accenture.com/us-en/about/company/coronavirus-business-economic-impact*

15 Accenture, "5 Priorities to Help Reopen and Reinvent Your Business" May, 2020, *https://www.accenture.com/_acnmedia/Thought-Leadership-Assets/PDF-3/Accenture-COVID-19-5-Priorities-To-Help-Reopen-And-Reinvent-Your-Business-v3.pdf*

16 Deloitte Insights, "Respond, Recover, Thrive IOM Advisory digital transformation webinar series," July 20, 2020, *https://www2.deloitte.com/content/dam/Deloitte/uk/Documents/digital-hub/ deloitte-uk-iom-future-of-work.pdf*

17 Andrew Blau, "Respond, Recover, and Thrive Beyond COVID-19", Deloitte Director Advisory, July/August, 2020, *https://www2.deloitte.com/us/en/pages/center-for-board-effectiveness/articles/respond-recover-thrive-beyond-covid-19.html*

18 Kantar, "Reframe, reskill, reset: how to win over the next 24 months", May 27, 2020, *https://www.kantar.com/inspiration/coronavirus/reframe-reskill-reset-cn*

19 Pam Kragen, "Pigs, goats and an alpaca are 'Zoom bombing' meetings from Ramona ranch during coronavirus lockdown", Los Angeles Times, April 28, 2020, *https://www.latimes.com/california/*

story/2020-04-28/pigs-goats-and-an-alpaca-are-zoom-bombing-meetings-from-ramona-ranch

20 Eric Grossman, "High-End Hotels Become Offices During Pandemic", Barrons, May 30, 2020, *https://www.barrons.com/articles/high-end-hotels-become-offices-during-pandemic-01590841040*

Chapter 3

21 David Green, "How Covid-19 is accelerating the Future of Work", LinkedIn, May 26, 2020, *https://www.linkedin.com/pulse/how-covid-19-accelerating-future-work-david-green/*

22 World Economic Forum, "Resetting the Future of Work Agenda: Disruption and Renewal in a Post-COVID World," White Paper, October 2020, *http://www3.weforum.org/docs/WEF_NES_Resetting_FOW_Agenda_2020.pdf*

23 AON, "Reprioritizing risk and resilience for a Post-Covid Future," March 2020, *https://www.aon.com/reprioritizing-enterprise-risk-management-resilience-and-insurance-covid19/index.html*

24 PWC, 2018 "Risk Review Study: Managing risks and enabling growth in the age of innovation", January 18, 2017, *https://www.pwc.com/sk/en/assets/PDFs/risk-in-review-2018.pdf*

25 Laura K. Murray, "How to Lead with Emotional Intelligence in the Time of COVID-19", April 21, 2020, Johns Hopkins School of Public Health Expert Insights, *https://www.jhsph.edu/covid-19/articles/how-to-lead-with-emotional-intelligence-in-the-time-of-covid-19.html*

26 Dale Buss, "Practicing High-EQ Leadership" Chief Executive,

September 24, 2020, *https://chiefexecutive.net/practicing-high-eq-leadership/*

27 Carol Stokes, "Workplace emotional intelligence during the global coronavirus outbreak" Brookings Blog, March 11, 2020, *https://www.brookings.edu/blog/techtank/2020/03/11/workplace-emotional-intelligence-during-the-global-coronavirus-outbreak/*

28 Jackie Wiles, "Gartner Top 3 Priorities for HR Leaders in 2021" Smarter with Gartner, October 23, 2020, *https://www.gartner.com/smarterwithgartner/gartner-top-3-priorities-for-hr-leaders-in-2021/*

29 Hank Tucker, "Coronavirus Bankruptcy Tracker: These Major Companies Are Failing Amid the Shutdown", Forbes, May 3, 2020, *https://www.forbes.com/sites/hanktucker/2020/05/03/coronavirus-bankruptcy-tracker-these-major-companies-are-failing-amid-the-shutdown/?sh=3fa1b1453425*

30 Lauren Thomas, "The 10 biggest retail bankruptcies of 2020", CNBC, December 26, 2020, *https://www.cnbc.com/2020/12/26/the-10-biggest-retail-bankruptcies-of-2020.html*

31 MHS, EQi-2.0 Emotional Intelligence Inventory Assessment, 2021, *https://storefront.mhs.com/collections/eq-i-2-0*

32 Punit Renjen, "The journey of resilient leadership," Deloitte Insights, December 2, 2020, *https://www2.deloitte.com/us/en/insights/economy/covid-19/how-leaders-help-business-thrive-post-covid-and-beyond.html*

33 US Bureau of Labor and Statistics, "Employment recovery in the wake of the COVID-19 pandemic" Monthly Labor Review, December 2020, *https://www.bls.gov/opub/mlr/2020/article/employment-recovery.htm*

34 Avie Schneider, "40.8 Million Out of Work in the

Past 10 Weeks– 26% Of Labor Force", NPR, May 28, 2020, *https://www.npr.org/sections/coronavirus-live-updates/2020/05/28/863120102/40-8-million-out-of-work-in-the-past-10-weeks*

35 Peter Deans, "The Big Covid-19 Blind Spot: Lack of Risk Management is Leaving us Wanting", Singularity Hub, April, 24, 2020, *https://singularityhub.com/2020/04/24/the-big-covid-19-blind-spot-lack-of-risk-management-is-leaving-us-wanting/*

36 Kerry Hearns-Smith, "Leading the Future of Work Transformations: 5 Key Strategy Elements", Association for Talent and Development, November 19, 2019, *https://www.td.org/insights/leading-future-of-work-transformations-5-key-strategy-elements*

Chapter 4

37 Annette LaPrade, Janet Mertens, Tanya Moore, and Amy Wright, "The Enterprise Guide to Closing the Skills Gap," IBM, 2019, *https://www.ibm.com/downloads/cas/EPYMNBJA*

38 World Economic Forum, "Jobs of Tomorrow Mapping Opportunity in the New Economy," White Paper Report, January 2020, *http://www3.weforum.org/docs/WEF_Jobs_of_Tomorrow_2020.pdf*

39 Ideal, "AI for Recruiting: A Definitive Guide for HR Professionals," 2020, *https://ideal.com/ai-recruiting/*

40 PWC Talent Trends 2020, "Upskilling: Building confidence in an uncertain world", Findings from PwC's 23rd Annual Global CEO Survey, 2020, *https://www.pwc.com/gx/en/ceo-survey/2020/trends/pwc-talent-trends-2020.pdf*

41 World Economic Forum, "Towards a Reskilling Revolution: Industry-Led Actin for the Future of Work", White Paper, January 2019, *https://www.weforum.org/whitepapers/towards-a-reskilling-revolution-industry-led-action-for-the-future-of-work*

42 Andrew Dyer, Susanne Dyrchs, Allison Bailey, Hans-Paul Burkner and J. Puckett, "Why It's Time to Bring Learning to the C-Suite" Boston Consulting Group, July 14, 2020, *https://www.bcg.com/publications/2020/why-it-is-time-to-bring-learning-to-the-c-suite*

43 LinkedIn Learning, "Workplace Learning Report: Skill Building in the New World of Work," LinkedIn Learning's 5th Annual 2021, *https://learning.linkedin.com/content/dam/me/business/en-us/amp/learning-solutions/images/wlr21/pdf/LinkedIn-Learning_Workplace-Learning-Report-2021-EN-1.pdf*

44 Bernard Marr, "The 9 Biggest Technology Trends That Will Transform Medicine and Healthcare In 2020", November 1, 2019, *https://www.forbes.com/sites/bernardmarr/2019/11/01/the-9-biggest-technology-trends-that-will-transform-medicine-and-healthcare-in-2020/?sh=1df9ee572cd3*

45 Josh Hrala, "CHROs: Here are the Top Five Companies Investing in Upskilling in 2020", CareerMinds Blog, November 11, 2020, *https://blog.careerminds.com/community/here-are-the-top-five-companies-investing-in-upskilling-in-2020*

46 Kate Whiting, "These are the top 10 job skills of tomorrow – and how long it takes to learn them" World Economic Forum, October 21, 2020, *https://www.weforum.org/agenda/2020/10/top-10-work-skills-of-tomorrow-how-long-it-takes-to-learn-them/*

Chapter 5

47 Deloitte Insights, "The social enterprise in a world disrupted Leading the shift from survive to thrive," 2021 Deloitte Global Human Capital Trends Report, 2020, *https://www2.deloitte.com/content/dam/insights/us/articles/6935_2021-HC-Trends/di_human-capital-trends.pdf*

48 The Business Roundtable, "Business Roundtable Redefines the Purpose of a Corporation to Promote An Economy That Serves All Americans," August 19, 2019, *https://www.businessroundtable.org/business-roundtable-redefines-the-purpose-of-a-corporation-to-promote-an-economy-that-serves-all-americans*

49 Lily Zheng, "We're Entering the Age of Corporate Social Justice," Harvard Business Review, June 15, 2020, *https://hbr.org/2020/06/were-entering-the-age-of-corporate-social-justice*

50 WorkHuman®, "Together we're pioneering a new way forward," WorkHuman Charter of Workplace Rights, 2021, *https://certified.workhuman.com/why-now/*

51 Holstee, "The Holstee Manifesto," 2020, *https://www.holstee.com/pages/manifesto*

52 PWC, "The way we work – 2025 and beyond", Future of Work Survey, 2017, *https://www.pwc.ch/en/publications/2017/the-way-we-work-hr-today_pwc-en_2017.pdf*

53 Kjaer Global & Unily, "Future of the Workplace 2030+", Unily Insights and Guides Future of Work, 2020

54 Angus Loten, "What Office Life Might Look Like in the Year 2030", Wall Street Journal, March 5, 2020, *https://www.wsj.com/articles/what-office-life-might-look-like-in-the-year-2030-11583362501*

Chapter 6

55 USA Today, "Good news in 2020? Yes, it's true! Here are 100 positive things that happened this year", USA Today staff, December 23, 2020, *https://www.usatoday.com/story/life/2020/12/23/good-news-2020-positive-stories-amid-coronavirus-election-celebrity-deaths/3921159001/*

56 Zack Guzman, "Robinhood CEO refutes GameStop hedge fund 'conspiracy theory' and reveals what actually happened," Yahoo Finance, January 21, 2021, *https://finance.yahoo.com/news/robinhood-ceo-refutes-game-stop-hedge-fund-conspiracy-theory-and-reveals-what-actually-happened-234600703.html*

57 Lilly Smith, "Five top designers imagine the workplace of 2040", Fast Company, January 29, 2020, *https://www.fastcompany.com/90450052/5-top-designers-imagine-the-workplace-of-2040*

58 American Psychological Association, "Stress in America 2020", National Mental Health Crisis Report, October 2020, *https://www.apa.org/news/press/releases/stress/2020/report-october*

59 Meaghan O'Neill, "The Design of Cities in the Year 2039", Architectural Digest, October 1, 2019, *https://www.architecturaldigest.com/story/future-of-design-cities*

60 Jeanne C. Meister and Robert H. Brown, "21 HR jobs of the Future", Harvard Business Review, August 12, 2020, *https://hbr.org/2020/08/21-hr-jobs-of-the-future*

61 Deloitte Insights, "The social enterprise in a world disrupted Leading the shift from survive to thrive," 2021 Deloitte Global Human Capital Trends Report, 2020, *https://www2.deloitte.com/content/dam/insights/us/articles/6935_2021-HC-Trends/di_human-capital-trends.pdf*

62 CBI Insights, "24 Industries and Technologies That Will Shape the Post-Virus World" Research Report, 2020

63 Natalie Morris, "The 10 surprising jobs that will be huge in 2050", METRO, April 29, 2019, *https://metro.co.uk/2019/04/29/the-10-jobs-arent-commonplace-yet-but-will-be-big-in-2050-9240386/*

64 Jess Joho, "58 things you probably forgot happened in 2020", Mashable, December 21, 2020, *https://mashable.com/article/what-happened-2020/*

Chapter 7

65 Colin C. Holley, Partner - Watt, Tieder, Hoffar & Fitzgerald LLP, "A Closer Look At The Coronavirus Pandemic As a Force Majeure Event," American Bar Association, March 31, 2020

66 Shana Lynch, "Andrew Ng: Why AI Is the New Electricity – A computer scientist discusses artificial intelligence's promise, hype and biggest obstacles." Insights By Stanford Business, March 11, 2017, *https://www.gsb.stanford.edu/insights/andrew-ng-why-ai-new-electricity*

67 Kelsey Snell, "What's Inside The Senate's $2 Trillion Coronavirus Aid Package", NPR, March 26, 2020, *https://www.npr.org/2020/03/26/821457551/whats-inside-the-senate-s-2-trillion-coronavirus-aid-package*

ABOUT THE AUTHOR

Dr. Terri Horton MBA, MA SHRM-CP, PHR
Workforce Futurist

Dr. Terri Horton is a workforce futurist and founder of FuturePath, LLC. She is a future of work expert. Her expertise sits at the intersection of the future of work, artificial intelligence, and the impact on business and people strategies. She is a consultant, corporate trainer, futurist coach, international speaker, and author that delivers high-impact and future-focused strategies and solutions for organizations, business professionals, and entrepreneurs. Her superpower is her unique ability to synthesize her combined background in corporate strategy, futuring and foresight, learning and organizational development, brand strategy, and higher education to deliver insights and results for clients to succeed in the accelerated unfolding of the future work.

Dr. Horton works with organizations to humanize the workplace by improving culture, worker experience, engagement, developing emotionally intelligent leaders and teams, crafting future-focused learning and reskilling strategies, and using artificial intelligence and data ethically and responsibly. She coaches business professionals and entrepreneurs to think, act and perform like futurists. She guides them in designing their futures with purpose and intention, grounded in foresight, resilience, hyper-relevancy, audacious boldness, and a commitment to unapologetically thriving on their terms.

Dr. Horton is a widely recognized thought leader on the future of work, an international speaker, and a subject-matter expert with two global research consultancies. She has provided strategic insights for the Pew Research Center, Forbes, and the Obama Foundation Scholars Program. She has provided training, coaching, and keynote speeches for Fortune 100 companies, nonprofits, professional associations, institutions of higher learning, government agencies, and international officials and executives from Asia, Europe, and Africa. She is a 2021 Forbes 50 over 50 nominee and a TEDx speaker. Dr. Horton's prior experience includes marketing and advertising leadership and executive roles with global media organizations and administrative roles in higher education.

Dr. Horton holds a doctorate in education focused on organizational change and leadership from the University of Southern California, a Master of Arts in organizational management, an MBA with a concentration in marketing, micro-credentials in artificial intelligence business strategy from Massachusetts Institute of Technology, and in data analytics and human resources from Cornell University. She is a Workhuman® Certified Professional, EQ-i 2.0 certified to assess, coach, and train leaders on emotional intelligence, holds SHRM-CP, PHR, and HCS human resource industry credentials, and is a university lecturer.

Dr. Horton is available for keynote speaking, consulting, executive coaching, corporate training, live and virtual events, board presentations, workshops, seminars, podcasts, book clubs, panels, and guest lecturing. Book Dr. Horton at *www.DrTerriHorton.com*

Stay informed or join the discussion:
Follow @DrTerriFuturist on Twitter
Follow @drterrihortonworkforcefuturist on LinkedIn

Made in USA - Kendallville, IN
73750_9780578249711
08.19.2022 1420